# A Practical Guide to Teaching Dance

ISBN-13: 978-1-905540-29-7
ISBN-10: 1-905540-29-9

Authors

**Fiona Smith**
**Lucy Pocknell**

The Association for Physical Education (afPE) is the physical-education subject association for all professionals with appropriate qualifications in physical education, sport and dance.

Room SC26
University of Worcester
Henwick Grove
Worcester
WR2 6AJ
Tel: 01905-855 584
Fax: 01905-855 594

Building 25
London Road
Reading
RG1 5AQ
Tel: 0118-378 6240
Fax: 0118-378 6242

Email: enquiries@afpe.org.uk
Website: www.afpe.org.uk

Published on behalf of afPE by

**Coachwise Business Solutions**
Coachwise Ltd
Chelsea Close
Off Amberley Road
Armley
Leeds LS12 4HP

Tel: 0113-231 1310
Fax: 0113-231 9606
Email: enquiries@coachwisesolutions.co.uk
Website: www.coachwisesolutions.co.uk

050389

# About the Authors

**Fiona Smith** is Principal Lecturer at Chelsea School, University of Brighton, where she is currently Programme Leader for Physical Education and Dance. Before joining the university, she worked as a dance artist in education and was a teacher of dance at various secondary schools. Fiona is an executive committee member of the National Dance Teachers Association (NDTA). Over the years, she has led numerous in-service courses for both new and experienced teachers on many aspects of dance, spanning Key Stage 3 through to examination work. She has a reputation for delivering high-quality teacher training that is challenging yet accessible and enjoyable. She has a particular interest in the teaching of dance composition and in raising the profile and status of dance for boys. She is Director of the all-male KICK-START Dance Company and the all-female FIDGIT Dance Company.

**Lucy Pocknell** is an Advanced Skills Teacher in Dance at Davison High School, Worthing, where she teaches at Key Stage 3, GCSE and A/S Level. She works closely with Chelsea School, University of Brighton as an initial teacher training mentor and guest lecturer. She is an executive committee member of the NDTA and an AQA moderator for GCSE Dance. In partnership with the local advisory service, she provides continuing professional development for teachers in primary and secondary schools in the Sussex area. In recent years, she has set up workshops for Gifted and Talented pupils in Year 9 and established a GCSE teachers' support group. She is well known locally and nationally for excellence in choreography and receives numerous invitations to share her work.

**The National Dance Teachers Association (NDTA)** is the voice for dance education. It supports teachers at all the key stages and at initial teacher training.

National Dance Teachers Association
PO Box 4099
Lichfield
WS13 6WX
Tel and fax: 01543-308 618
Email: office@ndta.org.uk
Website: www.ndta.org.uk

# Foreword

This resource represents not only a partnership between the Association for Physical Education (afPE) and the National Dance Teachers Association (NDTA), but the essential place of dance within schools. The physical education National Curriculum would be much poorer without dance which, of course, is also an integral part of schools' arts provision.

Yet, for many teachers, dance remains a challenge, as they often have not had the benefit of adequate dance preparation and may lack the confidence, skills or knowledge to make a start.

*A Practical Guide to Teaching Dance* is intended to support teachers, especially those working in the early years of secondary schools (Key Stage 3 in England, with children aged 11–14). It provides accessible help, with plenty of concrete ideas and schemes of work, thus building professional skills and understanding of how to structure and develop dance lessons effectively.

Dance is unique, as it offers young people creative, artistic and physical experience. Nationally, it is a fast-growing subject, especially in secondary schools, with the number of young people taking GCSE, AS/A2 Level and vocational examination courses in dance, increasing rapidly. There are many exciting dance initiatives in schools, involving teachers of physical education and, often, professional dance artists and agencies. At last, the outdated view that dance is only for girls is being swept away, as more and more schools are teaching dance to both boys and girls, in mixed or single-sex classes.

It is vital that more teachers develop their knowledge and skills in dance, so that both dance and students can flourish. With good teaching at this stage in secondary schools, students will be empowered to continue their dance involvement, whether into adult life or through developing the skills needed for progression into examination courses or performance.

Having made a start, many teachers find dance classes rewarding and satisfying, enjoying the enthusiasm and ideas that students themselves develop when given the opportunity to benefit from well-taught creative dance experiences.

We see this resource as an invaluable tool for encouraging high-quality dance learning and teaching in schools, in both arts and physical education curricula.

**Veronica Jobbins**
Chair, NDTA

National
Dance
Teachers
Association

**Margaret Talbot**
Chief Executive, afPE

# Contents

# Acknowledgements

We are grateful to the Association for Physical Education (afPE) and the National Dance Teachers Association (NDTA) for giving us the opportunity to share our work with fellow teachers in this way. For her invaluable advice, support and encouragement, we thank Judy Evans (Executive Member of the NDTA), who has guided us through this, our first publication. We are indebted to Graham Spacey for his technical know-how and creative flare in the filming of the DVD, to Steve Cridge, who produced the DVD, and to the professional team at Coachwise for their advice and work at the various stages of production.

A special note of thanks must go to Nick Carter, Debra Barrett and the many teachers, dancers and pupils who have generously given their time to assist us with the production of this resource (see below for the list of contributors).

Acknowledgment must also go to our families and friends who have shown patience and understanding during our efforts to complete this work.

Last, but definitely not least, we would like to pay tribute to the present and former students from Chelsea School, University of Brighton and the pupils from Davison High School, Worthing. They are our constant source of inspiration and the main reason we stay in our jobs, even after so many years!

**Contributors**

Photographers: Belinda Lawley (including cover images), Bob Seago, Barry Hope and Finn Taylor; dancers: Deb Barrett, Nick Carter, Kemal Dempster (street dancer), Yamuna Devi (Bollywood dancer), Daniella Grispino (street, Bollywood and contemporary dancer), Rosa Grispino (street dancer), Simmy Gupta (Bollywood choreographer), Brooke Milliner (street dancer); Sarah Dommett (glossary); Judy Evans (project management); students from the University of Brighton; pupils from Davison High School, Worthing; Chloe Kemp and pupils from Dorothy Stringer School, Brighton; Alison O'Neil and pupils from Homewood School, Tenterden; Mary Simmonds and pupils from Hailsham Community College, Hailsham; and Vicky Williams and pupils from Crookhorn School, Portsmouth.

The photos and video reproduced for Unit 3 were done so with the kind permission of Honda and Wieden & Kennedy.

The photographs in Unit 9 have been reproduced with the kind permission of Random Dance (Random Dance in Nemesis photographer: Ravi Depres).

| Key to Icons | | |
|---|---|---|
| Task | DVD (worksheets, teacher prompt sheets and video extracts) | Resources |
| Extension task | Video footage from other sources | Teacher note |

Teaching dance can sometimes be a daunting experience. In the process of compiling this resource, our main aim was to produce user-friendly guidance that addressed the most frequently asked questions and concerns raised by teachers:

- How do I come up with an idea?
- What music do I use?
- Where do I start when creating movement?
- How do I develop the idea within a lesson/across a unit?
- How do I get my pupils to be more creative?
- How do I ensure that learning is taking place?

The content and guidance provide you with answers to such questions and will help you plan and deliver high-quality dance. Using this resource and its accompanying DVD will develop your knowledge, skills and understanding of dance and the practice of dance teaching, and will enable you to build your confidence and competence as a practitioner. This handbook includes:

- guidance on planning a scheme and units of work
- an example scheme of work for Key Stage 3
- units of work for Years 7, 8 and 9
- learning and teaching resources
- teacher notes.

The materials have been 'tried and tested' and provide young people with a relevant and worthwhile experience. For each unit, we have developed a bank of learning and teaching resources, which are found on the accompanying DVD. The practical examples of movement phrases, video clips, worksheets (for pupils) and teacher prompt sheets (to aid teachers with ideas and provide information) all contribute to making your lessons fun, interesting and challenging.

Because the time allocated to dance varies greatly from school to school, this resource has been designed to provide flexibility for the teacher. It has not been broken down in a lesson-by-lesson format; instead, a series of progressive tasks are provided for you to select from, according to the interests and needs of your pupils and the time available.

Once you have decided which unit to teach, take the time to read the expectations provided at the start of the unit. Use these as the basis for writing your lesson objectives and outcomes. Where you do not have the time to teach all the tasks within the unit, ensure you select a range of performance, composition and appreciation tasks. While it is not essential that all three strands are given equal weighting within a single lesson, across the unit the balance between them should be relatively similar. A good dance lesson should have:

- a realistic, yet challenging and well-targeted set of learning objectives that are shared with the pupils
- links with previous lessons or include a clear introduction to a new area of study
- a warm-up that relates to the movement content and theme of the lesson
- a high level of practical activity
- a series of progressive and developmental tasks that remain focused on the objectives
- opportunities for pupils to rehearse and refine performance and choreography
- opportunities for pupils to observe, discuss and evaluate their own and others dances.

One of the unique features of this book is that, in addition to its practical content, it offers you ongoing professional training. A range of learning and teaching strategies common in successful dance practice is illustrated and a series of helpful teacher notes are included for your benefit. These notes steer you towards recognising and implementing good practice and, in so doing, advancing your knowledge and skills as a teacher of dance.

This handbook provides you with all the materials needed for an enjoyable and worthwhile dance experience, both for you and your pupils.

## Dance in the Curriculum

For the purpose of the English National Curriculum, dance is located within physical education (PE), providing an artistic and cultural dimension to the PE curriculum. It is acknowledged that dance is one of the major art forms that has strong links with drama, music and visual arts. Uniquely, dance provides the opportunity to use movement symbolically as a means of expression within a variety of cultural and aesthetic contexts.

Today, the provision of dance education varies greatly from school to school. In practice, dance remains located within different curriculum areas: as part of PE, as part of performing arts or as a subject in its own right, taught by teachers with a wide variety of training, experience and interests. Irrespective of where dance is located and who teaches it, an essential prerequisite for good practice is clarity of thinking about the contribution that dance makes to the curriculum. This understanding gives a sense of direction and purpose and underpins a teacher's choice of content and methodology.

The NDTA policy paper, 'Maximising Opportunity' (2004), states that:

> *Dance is a distinct area of experience fundamental to human culture and as such has the potential to offer unique learning opportunities within the school curriculum. As one of the major art forms, its intrinsic value lies in the possibilities it offers for the development of pupils' creative, imaginative, physical, emotional, and intellectual capacities.* ***Because of its physical nature, dance provides a means of expression and communication distinct from other art forms and because of its expressive and creative nature it stands apart from other physical activities.***
>
> *The practical, theoretical and contextual study of dance as an art form contributes to pupils' artistic, physical, aesthetic, cultural, and social development. It enables pupils to find their own voice as creator, performer and critic. Dance makes a special contribution to both physical and arts education, supports learning in other subjects and facilitates the development of key skills. It plays an important role in promoting physical fitness and well-being and contributes to pupils' understanding of how to maintain a healthy lifestyle.*

## Conceptual framework for teaching dance

When planning and delivering dance, consideration must be given to the three related strands of:

- **Performance** (the pupil as a dancer)
- **Composition** (the pupil as a choreographer)
- **Appreciation** (the pupil as a viewer and critic).

At times, greater emphasis may be given to one of the strands. For example, the majority of one lesson may be dedicated to using specific choreographic devices to explore movement material, while another may focus on recording and analysing pupil performance. Within each unit of work, however, these three strands should receive equal attention and be taught in an integrated way that acknowledges their interrelated nature.

### Performance

As the teacher, your role will be to:

- develop and extend pupils' movement vocabulary across various dance styles
- develop pupils' technical skills in dance
- develop pupils' expressive skills and ability to communicate choreographic intention
- develop pupils' ability to relate to other dancers, to the accompaniment and to their physical environment.

### Composition

As the teacher, your role will be to:

- provide pupils with interesting and inspiring starting points for dance
- develop pupils' ability to create original movement material related to the dance idea
- develop pupils' ability to adapt and develop movement material alone and with others
- develop pupils' ability to use choreographic devices to explore, develop and structure their ideas.

### Appreciation

As the teacher, your role will be to:

- develop pupils' ability to describe, analyse, interpret and evaluate their own and others' dance performance and composition
- develop pupils' ability to use dance-specific terminology when writing and speaking about dance
- encourage pupils to engage emotionally, imaginatively and intellectually with their own and others' dance works
- develop pupils' ability to recognise and understand the similarities and differences between dance genres and the work of different choreographers.

## Maximising Opportunities

The conceptual framework for teaching dance (performance, composition and appreciation) enables teachers to:

- deliver the National Curriculum
- prepare pupils for examination and vocational qualifications in dance
- provide a foundation for pupils to progress into further and higher education
- raise pupils awareness of how they can access dance as a creator, performer and viewer, beyond school and into adult life.

In providing a high-quality dance experience, teachers will also need to be aware of opportunities and new initiatives led by various arts and physical education organisations that help them to enrich the learning experiences of their pupils.

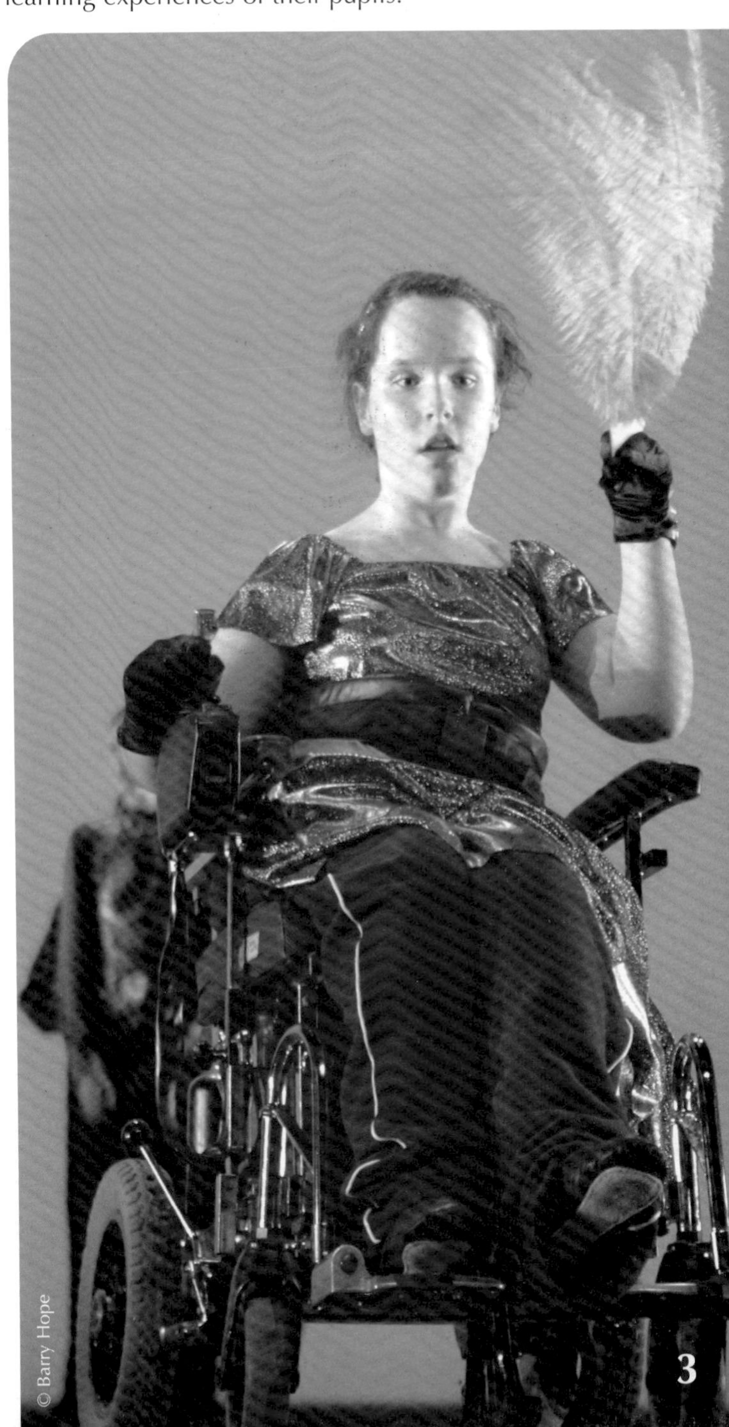

## Recognising High-quality Performance at Key Stage 3

| In high-quality performance, pupils will: | In performance that lacks high-quality, pupils will: | In order to achieve high-quality performance, pupils need: |
|---|---|---|
| show and maintain correct **posture** and **alignment** when dancing | have difficulty maintaining correct posture and, therefore:<br>• will show a slouched 'heavy' appearance<br>• will be unable to hold positions requiring any strength in the centre of the body | • to be taught what correct posture is<br>• to be taught why correct posture and alignment are important for effective jumping, balancing, turning, lifting and moving in and out of the floor and for the general aesthetic appearance of the dance<br>• the teacher to use imagery, such as 'pulling up' from the centre to improve posture<br>• the teacher to prompt continual self-check of posture<br>• to be given exercises or phrases of movement that focus on building core stability<br>• to view and analyse professional works that exemplify good posture |
| show clarity of **body shapes** and **extension** of the limbs | have difficulty showing clarity of shape and extension and, therefore:<br>• movements will appear 'unfinished' and will lack definition<br>• movements will not reach the extremities of the intended shape | • to see good examples of clear body shapes from the teacher, other pupils, and professionals on video and in photos, so that they have a 'model' to aspire to<br>• time to refine their movements so that they can concentrate on the detail of specific shapes<br>• the teacher to use imagery, such as that of elastic being pulled in both directions and extending beyond the ends of the fingertips and toes<br>• tasks which focus on opposites, such as feeling the difference between tension and relaxation |
| show good **coordination** when dancing with a sense of **fluency** in movement | have difficulty coordinating movement and, therefore:<br>• movement and timing will be disjointed and erratic<br>• there will be a sense of hesitancy when performing<br>• they will find it hard to concentrate on complex movement that requires many movements to be made simultaneously (eg with both arms and legs) | • movements to be built up progressively, such as learning foot patterns in isolation before adding arm movements<br>• time to consolidate and internalise the movement patterns<br>• to be taught what fluency is and how strategies, such as bending the knees and using momentum, can aid fluency<br>• the teacher to prompt continual self-check of fluency in all styles<br>• to view and analyse professional works which exemplify coordination and fluency |
| show good **spatial awareness** (eg clarity in directional changes and facings) and an awareness of other dancers when moving around shared space | have difficulty with changing directions and spacing and, therefore, will:<br>• have a limited sense of where they are in the space and, as a result, will get in the way of other dancers<br>• get confused easily when a dance requires constant changes of direction | • the teacher to provide points of reference in the room to help with directional clarity, such as for them to finish facing the windows or doors<br>• time to consolidate and internalise the spatial patterns<br>• to be given tasks which focus on changing spatial patterns and relationships |

<table>
<tr><th>In high-quality performance, pupils will:</th><th>In performance that lacks high-quality, pupils will:</th><th>In order to achieve high-quality performance, pupils need:</th></tr>
<tr><td>show good movement memory. Other pupils will often look to them for help with remembering dances. Pupils will be quick to pick up material and confident to work independently of the teacher</td><td>have difficulty remembering the sequencing of movement and, therefore:<ul><li>will often give up halfway through or need constant prompting about what comes next</li><li>will get frustrated with themselves and be reluctant to rehearse</li></ul></td><td><ul><li>the teacher to build up movement sequences, one phrase at a time</li><li>the teacher to use strategies which aid memory, such as naming sections of the dance or cueing key actions</li><li>the teacher to withdraw progressively from demonstrating and counting in front of the class</li><li>time to practise alone or with a partner to consolidate learning</li></ul></td></tr>
<tr><td>show a range of dynamics when dancing (eg contrasting movement qualities, such as different speeds and tensions)</td><td>have difficulty showing a range of dynamics in their performance and, therefore:<ul><li>their performance will lack expression and contrasting energies</li><li>all their movement will be at the same speed and intensity – fast is not fast enough, sharp is not sharp enough</li></ul></td><td><ul><li>to be taught about dynamics and how their appropriate use enriches performance and communication of the dance idea</li><li>the performance to be modelled, demonstrating a range of dynamic qualities clearly</li><li>the teacher to use a rich and descriptive dynamic vocabulary</li><li>the teacher to use intonation and expression to reinforce the desired qualities of movement</li><li>specific performance and composition tasks which focus on the use of contrasting dynamics</li><li>to view and analyse examples of professional works that exemplify contrasting dynamics</li></ul></td></tr>
<tr><td>show skill when performing the basic body actions, for example:<ul><li>– when jumping, they will show height, clarity of shape and control on landing</li><li>– when turning, they will show control, clarity of shape and effective use of focus to aid stability</li><li>– when gesturing, they will show clarity of action, dynamic and intention</li><li>– when balancing, passing through off-balance positions and when moving into and out of balance, they will show clarity of shape and control</li><li>– when travelling, they will show agility and ease in weight transference, from foot to foot and other body parts</li></ul></td><td>have difficulty when performing the basic body actions and, therefore:<ul><li>will struggle to get elevation when jumping, lack clarity of shape in the air and will perform landings that are heavy, awkward and flat-footed</li><li>there will be no judgment about how much effort is required to initiate turns, shapes during the turn will lack clarity, and they will stumble at the end of turns</li><li>the intention and shape of gestures will be vague and they will lack an appropriate dynamic and expressive quality</li><li>will struggle to maintain clarity of shape during stillness and will fall in and out of balances uncontrollably</li><li>will move uneasily around the space and attempts to transfer weight will lack fluency and control</li></ul></td><td><ul><li>to be taught techniques for jumping, turning, balancing, travelling and gesturing</li><li>tasks that focus on single actions in isolation before attempting to combine them into phrases</li><li>to experience performing the full range of actions through a variety of dance styles</li><li>technical principles to be continually reinforced throughout all phases of the lesson</li><li>to view and analyse professional works that exemplify a range of techniques</li></ul></td></tr>
<tr><td>show mobility in the joints and flexibility of the muscles, leading to full range of movement</td><td>have difficulty with flexibility and mobility and, therefore:<ul><li>some positions will be uncomfortable for them and they may be reluctant to persevere</li><li>their range of movement will be restricted, the sense of line will be distorted and actions will lack fluency</li></ul></td><td><ul><li>to be taught the importance of flexibility and mobility for the dancer</li><li>to be set short tasks which focus on developing flexibility and mobility</li><li>the teacher to correct individual pupils' alignment and body shape</li><li>to view and analyse professional dance works which exemplify how flexibility allows the dancer to fulfill the requirements of choreography</li></ul></td></tr>
</table>

| In high-quality performance, pupils will: | In performance that lacks high-quality, pupils will: | In order to achieve high-quality performance, pupils need: |
|---|---|---|
| show fluency, control and management of their own weight when **moving in and out of the floor** | have difficulty managing their own and others' weight and, therefore:<br>• transitional moments in and out of the floor will be clumsy and awkward. They will be prone to knock knees and elbows on the way down and struggle to get up | • to be taught techniques for moving in and out of the floor fluently and safely<br>• to learn these techniques slowly, progressing to full speed<br>• the teacher to demonstrate correct technique and point out potential hazards<br>• time to practise the floor material in isolation and then as part of the phrase |
| show sensitivity and appropriate expression when **communicating with other dancers** | have difficulty communicating with other dancers and, therefore:<br>• will appear self-conscious and find it hard to look at other dancers with an appropriate expression | • to understand what it is they are trying to communicate about the relationship between themselves and other dancers<br>• the teacher to establish an environment in which they can work sensibly and sensitively with other dancers<br>• to view and analyse professional works which exemplify aspects of effective communication between dancers |
| show skill in close-contact work and when **giving and taking weight** | have difficulty when working in close contact with other dancers and, therefore:<br>• other dancers will not feel safe being lifted by them and, when being lifted, there will be no sense of body tension<br>• will have a tendency to be 'silly' and embarrassed when asked to have physical contact with other dancers<br>• moments of contact will be clumsy and awkward | • the teacher to set clear expectations about how to behave when working with other dancers<br>• to work through a series of progressive tasks which build from non-contact through partial weight-bearing on to full weight-bearing<br>• to be taught techniques for safe lifting and catching<br>• to be taught that both dancers have an equal responsibility to ensure that a movement is executed safely and effectively<br>• to view and analyse professional work which exemplifies various aspects of contact work |
| show **musicality**, demonstrating a good sense of rhythm, phrasing and sensitivity to the mood and style of the music | have difficulty working with music and, therefore:<br>• movements will be out of time with the music<br>• rhythms will not be sustained<br>• movements will fail to reflect the style and mood of the accompaniment | • tasks that specifically focus on moving in time to contrasting pieces of music with different time signatures<br>• to be taught how to count in time with music<br>• the teacher to identify key points in the music that are cues for particular movements<br>• help with recognising the style and mood of the music<br>• time to practise so that timing becomes internalised |
| perform with a sense of **projection**, vitality and conviction. Their movements involve the whole body and show visible energy. They will understand the dance idea and show a commitment to it, which brings the dance to life | have difficulty projecting and showing visible energy and, therefore, will:<br>• lack physicality in their work – movements will appear marked with little physical exertion<br>• show limited commitment to the dance both physically and emotionally<br>• show no attempt to engage the audience | • to know what good projection looks like and be guided to see the difference between movement that is 'marked through' and movement that is performed with full energy and amplitude<br>• to recognise how dancers communicate and build up a rapport with an audience through focus, size of movement, energy, and sense of concentration and commitment to the dance idea<br>• to see live dance performances, ideally professional work or pupils from Key Stages 4 or 5, as projection and a sense of energy is often 'lost' on video<br>• the teacher to provide sufficient and various physical challenges as an integral part of all lessons<br>• to be told that dancing takes physical exertion and that they should be out breath after performing |

<table>
<tr><th>In high-quality performance, pupils will:</th><th>In performance that lacks high-quality, pupils will:</th><th>In order to achieve high-quality performance, pupils need:</th></tr>
<tr><td>use focus confidently and effectively</td><td>have difficulty using focus and, therefore, will:<ul><li>tend to look at the floor</li><li>make no attempt to include focus as part of their performance</li></ul></td><td><ul><li>to know the importance of focus and how it can help communicate an idea or enhance the design of movement</li><li>to view and analyse professional works that exemplify the effective use of focus</li><li>the teacher to continually 'point' out where focus should be directed for particular movements and why this will enhance communication of the dance idea</li><li>the teacher to consider the use of focus when creating phrases of movements to teach pupils</li></ul></td></tr>
<tr><td>be keen to share their work with others and perform with concentration and integrity.</td><td>have difficulty performing to others and, therefore, will:<ul><li>be reluctant to demonstrate or perform</li><li>not take it seriously when asked to share work</li><li>make no attempt to disguise mistakes</li><li>giggle and chat through performance</li><li>be prone to making derogatory remarks designed to disrupt or demean the atmosphere.</li></ul></td><td><ul><li>numerous opportunities to perform, ranging from showing a partner to showing a small group, half a class and then the whole class</li><li>the teacher to set clear standards and expectations about performing, such as holding starting and finishing positions, concentrating throughout and dancing without fidgeting</li><li>the teacher to establish a climate in which performing is a celebration of achievement</li><li>the teacher to ensure that pupils watch in an encouraging and supportive way so that performers feel at ease when dancing.</li></ul></td></tr>
<tr><td colspan="3">Throughout the key stage, pupils should have the opportunity to learn new, and to consolidate existing, technical and expressive skills through a range of dance styles.<br>Performing to peers and a wider audience both informally and formally will increase their confidence as performers.<br>Opportunities to see work live (examination work, local youth groups and professional artists) will enrich and enhance their appreciation of performance in dance.</td></tr>
</table>

## Recognising High-quality Composition at Key Stage 3

<table>
<tr><th>In a high-quality composition, pupils will:</th><th>In a composition that lacks high-quality, pupils will:</th><th>In order to achieve high-quality composition, pupils need:</th></tr>
<tr><td>create movement that relates to the dance idea in an appropriate style</td><td>find difficulty creating an original vocabulary in an appropriate style and, therefore will use:<ul><li>clichéd movement</li><li>'borrowed' movement vocabulary from an unrelated context or genre</li><li>their favourite movements, regardless of the appropriateness for the dance idea</li></ul></td><td><ul><li>help to see the unique movement potential of the initial stimuli</li><li>to be given, or helped to create, vocabulary in an appropriate style in order to build up their 'personal vocabulary bank'</li><li>to view and analyse professional works that exemplify how choreographers create movement that relates to a dance idea</li><li>to be encouraged to move out of their 'comfort zone' to experience different ways of moving</li></ul></td></tr>
<tr><td>explore and develop key motifs to a point that goes beyond the obvious</td><td>find difficulty exploring in depth and, therefore, will use:<ul><li>movements that are representational/mime-like</li><li>basic repetition and simplistic development of key motifs</li><li>movements that look like the first, most obvious response</li></ul></td><td><ul><li>to be set short choreographic tasks that focus on extending, altering and embellishing the initial motifs (development of the action, spatial, dynamic and relationship features)</li><li>to be given clear frameworks in which to improvise (a combination of narrow, highly structured tasks and broader, more open-ended tasks)</li><li>to view and analyse professional dance works that exemplify motif development</li><li>to work in an environment in which trial and error is encouraged and fear of failure is reduced</li></ul></td></tr>
</table>

| In a high-quality composition, pupils will: | In a composition that lacks high-quality, pupils will: | In order to achieve high-quality composition, pupils need: |
|---|---|---|
| use **contrasting dynamics** (qualities of movement) relevant to the dance idea | have difficulty using contrasting dynamics and, therefore, their movement will:<br>• lack physicality<br>• lack a contrast of qualities<br>• lack high points<br>• show rigid adherence to the pulse of music and limited rhythmic variation | • to know what dynamics are and how they help communicate a dance idea<br>• to have been set short choreographic tasks that focus on using and exploring a range of dynamics<br>• to view and analyse professional works that exemplify how the use of dynamics can help communicate a dance idea<br>• a bank of dynamic/qualitative vocabulary to draw upon |
| make effective use of **group designs**, numerical variations and physical relationships | have difficulty using a group of dancers effectively and, therefore will:<br>• use group designs which rely heavily on front-facing, two dimensional and symmetrical formations<br>• use predictable and repetitive canon<br>• show limited exploration of physical relationships<br>• use poor transitions | • to know how different formations, placement in the space and numbers of dancers suggest different meanings<br>• to take audience perspective into account when designing a dance<br>• to be set short choreographic tasks that focus on exploring aspects of formation, number and physical contact<br>• to view and analyse professional works that exemplify contrasting group designs, numerical variations and physical relationships<br>• to be taught the progressive skills of non-contact work through to weight-bearing<br>• to know what makes a good transition between movements and movement phrases, in order to maintain mood, style and expression |
| evoke **mood** and **emotion**. | have difficulty evoking mood and emotion and, therefore will:<br>• appear to be 'going through the motions'<br>• use bland and clinical movements with a sense of detachment<br>• lack of concentration<br>• lack integrity and understanding with regard to the choreographic intention. | • to be clear about the choreographic intention<br>• to be taught how choreographers use elements, such as focus, projection, space and contact to evoke mood and emotion<br>• to view and analyse a range of professional works that evoke contrasting moods/emotions. |
| Throughout the key stage, pupils should have the opportunity to experience working from a variety of stimuli (eg ideational, visual, kinesthetic, tactile, audio) and with contrasting accompaniment, from different musical genres. Opportunities to see work live (examination work, local youth groups and professional artists) will enrich and enhance their appreciation of composition in dance. | | |

## Recognising High-quality Appreciation at Key Stage 3

| In high-quality appreciation, pupils will: | In appreciation that lacks high-quality, pupils will: | In order to achieve high-quality appreciation, pupils need: |
|---|---|---|
| **identify** and **describe** in detail aspects of their own and others' work using appropriate vocabulary when writing and talking about dance | have difficulty identifying and describing in detail and will:<br>• require specific guidance about what to look for<br>• offer descriptions that are brief and lack specificity<br>• require continual prompting to extend their answers and find the right words to use | • to hear the teacher modelling detailed answers, using appropriate vocabulary<br>• to be given specific vocabulary to use when describing aspects of performance and composition<br>• the teacher to be continually 'pointing out' key aspects of performance and composition<br>• plenty of opportunities to practice talking about dance with a partner, in small groups and in front of the class<br>• key words to be displayed around the dance space as a point of reference<br>• to recognise that dance is frequently described in terms of action, spatial, dynamic and relationship features |
| **analyse** in detail component parts of their own and others' work showing an understanding of context and style | have difficulty analysing in detail and, therefore will:<br>• show confusion over the difference between action, spatial, dynamic and relationship features<br>• offer random comments that suggest lack of understanding of key concepts within given criteria<br>• offer superficial responses<br>• struggle to see the need for detailed analysis and how this can help their understanding and be applied to their own work | • the process of analysis to be embedded within the teaching of performance and composition, alongside discrete viewing tasks<br>• to be given frameworks for dance analysis that help pupils distinguish between the components of dance<br>• to be given simple to complex analysis tasks that focus on specific aspects of performance or choreography<br>• the teacher to provide information and guidance about stylistic features of different dances<br>• help in recognising similarities and differences between works they have seen and experienced |
| give articulate and perceptive responses and **interpret** what they see in relation to the dance idea and how this idea has been explored. They will be able to explain how and why various action, spatial, dynamic and relationship features, plus elements of production, have been selected in the creation and performance of a dance | find difficulty interpreting and, therefore will:<br>• struggle to offer suggestions relating to what movements might represent within a dance<br>• be challenged by questions that require them to go beyond description to suggest how and why<br>• be unable to see the link between the components of dance, or elements of production, and how these help communicate the dance idea | • to be given contextual information related to aspects such as the theme, inspiration, era, place, choreographer and style, in order to engage pupils on a cerebral and emotional level, as well as a physical level<br>• to be given time to prepare their answers to allow them to speak fluently and articulately<br>• the teacher to be persistent and supportive when encouraging pupils to give detailed answers<br>• questions that constantly require them to consider the movement vocabulary, choreographic devices and elements of production in relation to the dance idea<br>• to be encouraged to use a rich and expressive language that captures meaning, mood and feelings, in addition to technical and descriptive vocabulary |
| be thoroughly **engaged** and captivated by the work, and keen to offer personal opinions and emotional responses to what they have seen or participated in. Their responses will make a connection between how they feel and what evoked those feelings | • appear disinterested and detached from the work being viewed<br>• have few opinions about the work<br>• need encouragement to share their response with the group | • the teacher to be enthusiastic, energetic and inspired by the theme/work undertaken<br>• to see that the teacher values their opinions and praises pupils who are willing to share thoughts and feelings with the group<br>• to work in a supportive and open environment in which they feel comfortable to express how they feel about what they have seen |

<table>
<tr><th>In high-quality appreciation, pupils will:</th><th>In appreciation that lacks high-quality, pupils will:</th><th>In order to achieve high-quality appreciation, pupils need:</th></tr>
<tr><td>accurately evaluate their own and others' work, based on specific criteria given by the teacher, in relation to performance and composition</td><td>have difficulty accurately evaluating and, therefore will:<br>• make random comments that do not necessarily relate to the focus of the evaluation task<br>• be unable to make a judgement about the quality of what they see and its effectiveness<br>• have low expectations of their own and others' abilities and therefore are too easily content with what they see</td><td>• opportunities to evaluate in writing and orally<br>• to experience a range of learning and teaching strategies to develop evaluative skills, such as reciprocal teaching episodes, self-check sheets and video analysis<br>• a realistic number of clear, well-focused criteria, based on aspects of performance and composition<br>• to view what they are evaluating more than once, in order to make fair and worthwhile judgements<br>• to practise giving formative and summative evaluations of their own and others' work, throughout a unit</td></tr>
<tr><td>give and receive critical feedback with honesty and sensitivity, understanding that the most effective comments are based on objective features of the work or aspects of performance/composition.<br>They will be able to accurately identify strengths and weaknesses in their own and others' work and suggest effective and realistic ways to improve.</td><td>• lack sensitivity when giving feedback to peers; often their responses will be personal or negative in tone<br>• provide feedback that lacks focus and specificity<br>• offer limited suggestions for improvement.</td><td>• to be introduced to the etiquette of criticism, such as the need for a balance between the identification of strengths/areas for development and the tone with which criticism should be given<br>• to be taught the value of critical comments, in order to improve work and deepen understanding<br>• to be taught to accept both positive and corrective comments<br>• the teacher to provide clear guidance on what to look for<br>• to be taught how to phrase feedback so that it is positive and corrective and includes specific and manageable targets<br>• to be given time to put the corrective feedback into practice and then to receive further feedback on progress<br>• the opportunity to move beyond their immediate friendship group to practise giving feedback, as this requires greater objectivity and courage.</td></tr>
<tr><td colspan="3">Throughout the key stage, pupils should have the opportunity to observe regularly and comment on dance work, other than their own and that of their classmates. Observing and commenting on short extracts of professional works should be integrated within the teaching of units of work.<br>Opportunities to see work live (examination work, local youth groups and professional artists) and to talk and write about what they have seen will enrich and enhance their knowledge and understanding.</td></tr>
</table>

## The Scheme of Work

The Key Stage 3 scheme that follows contains nine units of work: three for Year 7, three for Year 8 and three for Year 9. The units within the scheme, when taught in sequence, are designed to offer a broad, balanced and progressive dance experience.

To aid your understanding of the scheme, and guide you through future planning, the following key points should be noted:

- **Each unit of work identifies the knowledge, skills and understanding to be taught in relation to the three strands of performance, composition and appreciation** (these are identified at the beginning of each unit as a set of learning expectations). An overview of all unit expectations within the Key Stage 3 scheme can be found on the DVD.

It is important to note that the knowledge, skills and understanding should be considered as separate from the context for learning. The same knowledge, skills and understanding can be taught 'through' a variety of styles and dance ideas. The teacher needs to realise that it is the context for learning that engages pupils; therefore, they must select appropriate contexts that will suit and inspire their own pupils, as well as ensure that the desired knowledge, skills and understanding have been addressed.

- **Equal attention is given across the scheme to learning that is related to performance, composition and appreciation.**

In practice, the three strands are taught in an integrated way. However, at times, greater or lesser attention may be given to one of the three strands.

- **The knowledge, skills and understanding in relation to the three strands of performance, composition and appreciation progress within the scheme.**

Each year, there is the opportunity to revisit and consolidate existing knowledge, skills and understanding, as well as to embark upon new, more advanced challenges.

For example, in relation to performing:

- in Unit 1, pupils learn to work with accurate timing in close proximity to a partner
- in Unit 3, pupils learn to initiate each others' movement by using brief moments of contact
- in Unit 6, pupils learn to take their partner's whole body weight.

In relation to composition:

- in Unit 1, pupils learn to develop their work through the use of choreographic devices, such as leading/following and question/answer
- in Unit 4, pupils learn to develop their work through the use of choreographic devices, such as shadowing, complementing and overlapping, within a more abstract context
- in Unit 8, pupils learn to develop their work through the use of choreographic devices, such as complex combinations of lifting, dragging, pulling and pushing in small groups.

- **The content takes account of pupils' growing physical, emotional, intellectual and social maturity.**

For example, the units of work based on Guernica and My Name is Cocaine require the pupils to interact with one another in a sophisticated way. Pupils will also consider issues of social and historical importance, typically beyond their immediate life experiences. In contrast, at the start of the scheme, Cartoon Capers provides a fun and instantly accessible context for learning.

- **There is use of a variety of stimuli.**

The scheme contains a variety of **visual**, **auditory**, **ideational** and **kinaesthetic** starting points (stimuli), designed to inspire and engage pupils. For example, paintings, poems, graffiti art, professional dance works, contemporary issues and historic events are used throughout.

It is important to note that the contexts for learning (dance styles and ideas) are selected to generate a contrasting movement vocabulary across the scheme. In addition, each idea requires pupils to engage in a different way, physically and emotionally.

The majority of units use multiple stimuli to spark pupils' imagination and bombard them with a wealth of ideas to inspire movement.

- **There is use of a variety of accompaniment.**

Throughout the scheme, pupils are given an opportunity to dance to music of different styles, for example, popular, classical, atmospheric and music from different cultures. It is important for the teacher to realise the significance that pupils place on enjoying the music. Teachers, however, need to broaden pupils' musical taste and guide them to see the appropriateness of music outside popular culture.

- **Frequent reference is made to professional dance works.**

Reference to professional dance works permeates the scheme, sometimes to briefly exemplify features of performance and composition, or as the main focus and starting point for a unit. Where reference is made to professional dance works, it is not with the intention of replicating the material but as a springboard for pupils' own work. Pupils should come to know professional dance artists and their work in the same way that they learn about famous authors, painters, musicians and sportsmen and women.

- **Units include opportunities for learning across the curriculum.**

Inherent within performing, composing and appreciating dance, is the opportunity to address broader dimensions of the curriculum, such as literacy, numeracy, ICT, PSHE, citizenship and pupils' creativity and thinking skills. For example, within the Urban unit (Unit 5), pupils will consider how the discipline required to master extreme physical challenges may impact on self-esteem. Pupils are also asked to consider the tragic and controversial events of Guernica and to draw parallels with contemporary incidents from around the world.

- **Units include opportunities for cross-curricular learning.**

Several units within the scheme take a cross-curricular theme, such as the social issue of drug awareness, the study of a famous painting, or the historic study of Roman gladiators, as the main context for learning. While not the primary focus of other units, opportunities can still occur to address cross-curricular matters. It is important that the teacher takes full advantage of these and plans for their inclusion.

- **Units include a range of learning and teaching strategies.**

Each unit includes various ways to learn about performing. For example, pupils will learn technical exercises, phrases of movement and short dances, then practise and refine their dances to perform to their peers. In composing, pupils will learn to improvise within given frameworks to create original movement material, then to adapt, develop and structure their own and given material into meaningful dances. In learning about appreciation, pupils will observe and comment on their own and others' dances, including professional works, interpreting and judging what they see and then give informed feedback.

# Unit 1: Cartoon Capers (Year 7)

## About the Unit

This unit is inspired by Looney Tunes Cartoons. Pupils will explore common features of cartoons, such as the suspension of reality, the indestructible nature of the characters, the sticky situations they encounter and how, eventually, good always triumphs over bad.

This theme is accessible, great fun and will instantly engage the pupils. The content is action-packed and demands a high level of energy, plus pupils will have the opportunity to use their imagination to create and interpret various cartoon storylines. Throughout the unit, pupils work on creating and performing two short dances based on cartoons.

The unit focuses on refining and developing technical skills in a variety of basic whole-body actions. The attention to characterisation and concentration on extreme dynamic contrasts develops pupils' expressive skills.

Choreographically, pupils concentrate on creating and developing movements that relate to the themes of the two cartoons, structuring a simple narrative duet and using dynamic contrast to enhance communication of the dance idea. As they work, they identify and interpret the storyline of various cartoons, explain their choice of actions in relation to the dance idea and describe what they see using a descriptive and dynamic vocabulary.

While a key priority for this unit is enjoyment, there is a danger that, when teaching work of this nature, it can become mime-like or slapstick. Pupils may need to be constantly reminded of the difference between dance and mime, and taught how to make actions more dance-like. Therefore, this unit includes choreographic tasks based on devices, such as freeze frame, slow motion, enlargement and developing the rhythmic phrasing of actions, which will help pupils understand the concept of abstraction.

## Resources

**Music**

- 'One Step Beyond', 'Nutty Themes' and 'Fireball XL5' by Madness from the album, *Madness: Business* (Virgin Records, 1993).
- Looney Tunes' *The Wacky Cartoon Music Companion* (1998) (product code: DWCD0254) (includes traditional cartoon music and sound effects).

**Video**

- *Looney Tunes Bumper Edition, Volume 7* from Warner Bros Family Entertainment (1998) (product code: SO16009) (most other Looney Tunes cartoons would also be a suitable substitute).

**Additional Resources and Information**

- For downloadable images of cartoon characters, go to www.looneytunes.warnerbros.co.uk
- For fun sound effects and to hear short soundbites of popular characters speaking, go to www.nonstick.com/sounds
- For graphics, storyline scripts and lists of special effects, go to www.cerbslar.com/tcc/crash_course

## Expectations

### Performance

- **Demonstrate technical skill in the five basic body actions, such as jumping, turning, gesturing, balancing and travelling** (eg height, clarity of shape in the air and a controlled landing when jumping).
- **Demonstrate complex combinations of body actions with fluency and control** (eg performing a phrase of movement that includes and links together smoothly jumping, rolling and balancing).
- **Demonstrate clarity and precision in the use of contrasting dynamics** (eg the difference between fast, explosive action and smooth, sustained action).
- **Demonstrate a sense of musicality and rhythm, alone and in time with a partner** (eg working on the beat and maintaining a pulse, rhythmic accuracy and phrasing).
- **Demonstrate facial expressions that help communicate the idea** (eg shock, fear and surprise).

### Composition

- **Create movements that relate to the theme and use a variety of body actions and dynamics** (eg stopping abruptly and then jumping and rushing away to show shock and fear).
- **Develop and adapt their movements** (eg use freeze frame, rhythm and enlargement).
- **Apply basic relationship devices to help tell the story** (eg leading, following, overtaking, questioning and answering).

### Appreciation

- **Identify key characteristics of cartoons and their main action and dynamic content** (eg indestructible characters that fly, fall and rebound).
- **Use appropriate terminology when analysing and describing their own and others' work** (eg abstraction, repetition and focus).
- **Comment on the work of others, identifying strengths and areas for development** (eg acknowledging moments where the characterisation is well expressed and highlighting moments that need greater attention to dynamic clarity).

## Cartoon Capers

This unit culminates in two short duets, each imitating separate cartoons. The first includes set material with choreographic developments, while the second is based on the pupils' interpretation of a comic-strip storyboard.

### Task 1

**Introducing dance one**

a) Play cartoon, Tweety in *Dog Pounded,* as pupils enter. Ensure the task below is written on the board:

*Think of four things that happen in most cartoons (eg characters appear to die but then come back to life).*

b) Facilitate discussion of the common characteristics of cartoons. Key points to be listed on the board (one example is: reality is suspended – the characters can do things that humans can not).

Teacher Prompt Sheet: Cartoons – Common Characteristics.

### Task 2

**Video observation**

Watch second cartoon: Tweety and Sylvester in *The Jet Cage.*

Together, with pupils, complete the worksheet identifying the storyline. Pay particular attention to the use of action and dynamic language.

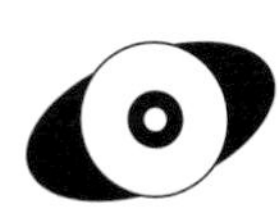

Pupil Worksheet: What Happens to Sylvester?

### Task 3

**Learning the set material: Chase Phrase**

Having identified the nature of cartoons, the typical storylines, their action and dynamic content, pupils are now ready to apply this to the dance context. To ensure that pupils understand how to abstract movement (taking it beyond slap-stick and mime), begin the practical work within this unit by teaching set material. This material illustrates the key characteristics identified previously and will form the beginning section in the first two cartoons that pupils will go on to create and develop.

Pupils learn the set 'Chase phrase' either from you or directly from the video. This material illustrates the key characteristics identified previously and will form the beginning section in the first of two cartoons that pupils will go on to create and develop.

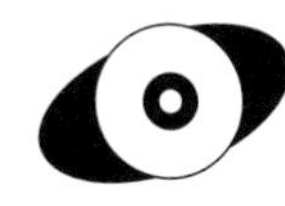

Video Extract: Set Material – Chase Phrase.

**Using set material**

**Using set material (for instance, a prescribed phrase of movement usually choreographed by the teacher) is a popular and valuable teaching strategy because it:**

- gives an idea of the style of the dance to be created
- broadens pupils' movement vocabulary
- provides the opportunity to concentrate on technical and expressive skills
- provides material that can be used as a foundation for composition work
- allows the teacher to dictate the structure/pace and direction of the lesson.

### Task 4

**Refining set material**

Having been taught the set material, time should now be dedicated to practising and refining the technical and expressive skills inherent within the phrase.

Give pupils structured practice time to focus on:

- technical skill (eg jumping high and landing with control, showing precision and speed when changing direction, and linking movements within the phrase smoothly)
- dynamic contrasts (eg the difference between the powerful and explosive jump and the slow, melting collapse to the floor)
- clarity of shape (eg the wide, broad and open shape on hitting the wall and the twisted torso at the start of the suspension, leading into the cartoon run).
- musicality (eg accurate rhythmic phrasing).
- expression and characterisation (eg matching facial expressions to each incident throughout the phrase and performing with a sense of energy and enthusiasm).

**Using reciprocal teaching**

Reciprocal teaching is a valuable strategy to use when refining set material. Providing pupils with simple criteria as the basis for offering feedback to a partner, reinforces key technical and expressive points and maximises the amount of feedback each child receives.

This strategy is most valuable when used on a short phrase of movement or to focus on particular moments that are technically challenging.

## Task 5

### Adapting the set material to work with a partner

Now that pupils know and can perform the material confidently, they are ready to begin personalising, adapting and developing it to work with a partner.

Using the set material, compose a short duet that communicates various aspects of two friends being chased.

a) Lead the discussion about the choreographic intention and create a list of possible scenarios. For example, the friends could:
   - beckon one another to safety
   - hold hands as they run or help one another up from the floor
   - look out for themselves, by trying to get ahead of their partner
   - experience the dangers either at the same time or successively.

b) Use two pupils to demonstrate how the choreographic devices of leading, following and overtaking, question and answer, canon, unison and repetition can be used to communicate the dance idea. You can use adaptations and developments of the set material (eg at the start, dancer A runs, stops, turns and beckons to dancer B. They jump, holding hands. In canon, dancer A suspends into a cartoon run, followed by dancer B).

c) Pupils can begin to explore the task. Periodically, stop the class to share good examples and to reinforce the key choreographic devices.

d) Pupils should structure and refine their duet and prepare for performance. Split the group so that half the class watches the other half of the class. The observers should watch an allocated duet and comment on how the choreographic devices help communicate aspects of the relationship between the two friends (eg when the pair held hands and looked shocked at the same time, it emphasised their predicament).

## Task 6

### Extending the duet material

By this stage, the pupils will be keen to add their own ideas. The following task gives pupils more opportunity to create their own movement vocabulary from options provided by you.

a) Extend the duet phrase by depicting the following storyline. Create a short transition that will lead into this section of the cartoon.

   Dancer A: Hits an imaginary wall and melts down slowly.

   Dancer B: Stops abruptly short of the wall and watches. Dancer A staggers to his feet and spins around in a daze.

   Dancer B: Laughs and points at dancer A in an exaggerated manner.

   Dancer A: Gestures angrily and gives chase.

b) Extend the phrase further by adding at least two scenarios from the list on the worksheet. Items from the Cartoon Cupboard, also identified on the worksheet, may also be used to make the dance more exciting.

Pupil Worksheet: Ideas for Your Chase.

UMBRO

### Task 7

**Dance two: Composing a short duet**

This task asks pupils to create their own comic strip and show they understand abstract movement.

Pupil Worksheet: Comic Strip Storyboard.

a) Explain how to use the storyboard and ask pupils to reflect on how previous material within the unit was abstracted.

b) Pupils begin the process of devising movement for their comic strip. During this exploratory phase, provide feedback to both individual pairs and the whole group. Periodically, the whole class should stop to watch good examples and to be introduced to new strategies to be used within their developing duets, for instance:

- **enlarging movements** (eg altering the size of some actions by using greater amounts of space, involving the whole body, or taking movements into the air and onto the floor)
- **using freeze-frame moments** (eg pausing on key moments, such as just before a punch makes an impact, or suspending and holding the reaction to an explosion. Facial expressions can enhance the 'photographic' moment)
- **using repetition** (eg performing the same action a number of times to emphasise a point. Repetitions can be identical or can show development)
- **developing rhythmic phrasing** (eg building rhythmic moments within the dance, such as giving travelling movements a clear rhythmic structure that is in time with the music).

c) Give pupils time to refine their duets, ready to perform to another pair. Particular attention should be paid to dynamic contrasts and characterisation.

Pupil Worksheet: Action/Dynamic words

### Task 8

**Performing the duet**

a) Each pair performs their duet to another pair.

Observers should:

- comment on how contrasting dynamics have been used to communicate the storyline successfully
- identify points for development relating to dynamic contrast and characterisation.

b) Each pair is given time to work on the targets set by their observers.

### Task 9

**Performing Cartoon Capers to the whole group**

**Performance behaviour and audience etiquette**

It is a valuable experience for pupils to perform to one another and observe the work of their peers. However, it can also prove to be a little intimidating, for example, when pupils are expected to perform in individual groups in front of the whole class. In order to build confidence in performing, it is important that you structure opportunities carefully, and ensure there is plenty of time to refine and rehearse their work. Pupils can only perform with confidence when they are familiar with their dance.

Pupils should be taught **performance skills**. For example:

- stillness at the beginning and end of a performance
- concentration throughout their performance
- attention to focus and projection.

Pupils should be taught **performance behaviour**. For example, while performing they must not:

- chew or eat
- talk, giggle or laugh
- rearrange their clothing
- adjust their hair.

Pupils should be taught **audience etiquette**. For example, they must:

- give their full attention and concentration to the performance they are observing
- be supportive and encouraging of the other dancers
- give positive and constructive feedback.

# Unit 2: Bollywood (Year 7)

## About the Unit

This unit takes, as its starting point, Bollywood-style dancing. The unit acknowledges the growing popularity of Bollywood films, and illustrates how one aspect of Indian culture is becoming more mainstream. It provides opportunities for pupils to experience a lively and expressive dance form that mixes aspects of a traditional dance with modern-day influences.

The unit focuses on basic aspects of Bollywood technique and expression, such as posture, grace, hand movements, and on portraying energy and emotion.

Choreographically, pupils create and structure movements in a Bollywood style, and take inspiration from the instructions given by a professional dancer and choreographer and the words and rhythm of the music. As they work, pupils analyse basic action and spatial, dynamic and relationship components to identify the stylistic features of Bollywood dancing and choreography. Consideration is given to understanding the importance of dancing in Bollywood films.

Bollywood dancing is a wonderful fusion of various Indian and western dance forms, such as Bhangra (a lively form of dance that originated in the Punjab region of southeast Asia; it is often used as a form of celebration) and hip hop (an urban cultural movement that began in New York, which involves rapping, DJing, graffiti art, beat boxing and break dancing), with a touch of pure Bollywood cheese to top it of! As the teacher, you may feel that this material is not within your cultural experience and, therefore, you don't have the knowledge or skills to teach this unit in a meaningful and authentic way. However, providing you are honest with the pupils about your limitations, and make the effort to use available resources to support your teaching, there is no reason why your pupils should not have an enjoyable and worthwhile learning experience.

It is a good idea to approach this unit as a joint learning experience, where both you and the pupils watch, listen, read, copy and explore together to discover the essence of Bollywood dance. Ideally this unit would be enriched if pupils had the opportunity to work with and see trained Bollywood dancers live.

### Resources

**Music**

- Captain Bhangra Da, Partners in Rhyme, found on *Rough Guide to Bhangra Dance* (Rough Guides, 2006).
- Punjabi wedding song (found on *Bride and Prejudice* (Casablanca, 2005) film soundtrack album).
- *Indestructible Asian Beats* (Manleca Records, 2001) by various artists.

**Video/DVD**

- *Bride and Prejudice* (Miramax Home Entertainment, 2005).
- *Bollywood Workout* (Momentum Pictures Home Entertainment, 2002) by Honey Kalaria.

**Websites**

- www.nutkhut.net

**Additional Resources and Information**

- www.bollywoodworld.com
- www.4x4dhol.com/bhangra.htm

## Expectations

### Performance

- **Demonstrate a sense of rhythm, musicality and energy, when performing Bollywood-style movements** (eg awareness of timing, phrasing and downward accent and a lively energetic approach).
- **Demonstrate grace, elegance and expression in movement, particularly when performing hand gestures** (eg precision and detail in the use of the wrists and fingers, appropriate focus and facial expressions and the smooth, fluid use of the whole body).
- **Demonstrate spatial awareness when performing as a group** (eg maintaining group formations while dancing, and control when moving through and around other dancers).

### Composition

- **Select, order and structure movements in a Bollywood style, showing various group formations and pathways** (eg the use of block and circle formations, diagonals, and curved and zigzag pathways).
- **Create movements in a Bollywood style that physically interpret given lyrics** (eg movements that reflect the action, relationships and emotions stated in the words, such as love, hatred and anger).

### Appreciation

- **Identify key stylistic features of performance and choreography in Bollywood films** (eg how the meanings of songs are interpreted in dance, and how films are characterised by glamorous costumes, lots of colour and extravagant sets, and a fusion of dance styles such as Bhangra and Hip Hop).
- **Analyse professional examples of Bollywood dancing and use this to set realistic targets for improvement** (eg show a greater range of movement in the shoulders and a stronger forceful downward accent on the Bhangra steps).
- **Draw and describe key group formations and pathways** (eg use diagrammatic form and appropriate vocabulary to illustrate pathways, such as 'straight', 'curved' and 'zigzag', and use appropriate spatial vocabulary, such as 'towards', 'passing' and 'diagonal').

## Bollywood

This unit culminates in a group dance with three sections. The first section includes adaptations of taught material. In the second section, pupils learn individual steps as demonstrated by a professional dancer (from the DVD). In the final section of the dance, pupils devise their own lyrics and associated movements into a Bollywood-style routine.

### Task 1

**Introducing the dance idea**

a) Organise pupils to watch a dance scene from the Bollywood film *Bride and Prejudice* (5mins and 35secs from the opening credits). Facilitate introductory question time to find out what pupils already know about Bollywood dancing. Some examples of questions include:

- Can anyone name the dance style?
- Has anyone seen anything similar before? If so, can they explain it?
- Has anyone done any Bollywood dancing or does anyone know anybody that has?
- What are your first impressions of the dancing in the film?
- How would you describe the dancing in the film?

Feed in basic facts about Bollywood dancing.

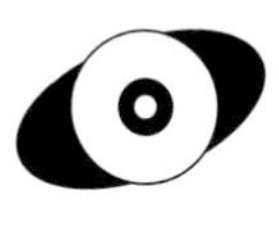

Teacher Prompt Sheet: Key Features of Bollywood Dancing.

### Task 2

**Learning a set Bollywood routine**

Video Extract: Set Material – Bollywood Routine.

To help with the stylisation of movement, you need to continually reinforce the key teaching points as identified in the commentary on the video.

**Getting moving**

When introducing a new idea, it is essential that pupils understand what they will be doing and why they will be doing it. Moreover, pupils will also need to understand the context of the work and the key stylistic features. It is important to realise, however, that much of this information can be permeated by and delivered through practical work. Avoid the tendency to talk for too long, especially on the first lesson of a unit. Give pupils the basic information they need and then get them moving. Once pupils have experienced the style physically, they will be more receptive to factual information, analytical tasks and the importance of teaching points relating to style.

### Task 3

**Analysing *Bride and Prejudice* routine and target-setting to improve pupil performance**

a) Ask pupils to describe what is good about the way the dancers move. Using this discussion as a basis, ask pupils to identify two things they are going to improve for their next performance of the set Bollywood routine.

b) In pairs, ask pupils to share their areas for improvement with one another, and then take time to practice and help one another to implement their improvements.

c) Lead the whole class through the performance of the set material once more.

d) In groups of six, ask the pupils to adapt the Bollywood routine to show at least two different group formations (eg a rectangle or two parallel diagonal lines).

e) Pupils should now practise the adapted material, concentrating on maintaining formations as they dance.

### Task 4

**Watching Bollywood-style routines by Yamuna Devi**

The video extract on the DVD illustrates Bollywood dancing at an advanced level. It sets the scene for pupils to create their own routines, using simplified versions of the type of movement demonstrated.

Video Extract: Example Material – Bollywood-style Routine.

### Task 5

**Creating a section for the Bollywood Routine**

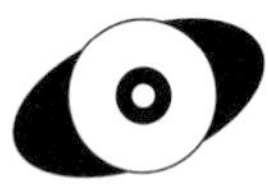

Video Extract: Example Material – Bollywood Steps.

a) Just show the first step (on the video extract, Bollywood steps) to your pupils. Help them to replicate what they have seen on the video. Assist your pupils with strategies for watching extracts (eg advise pupils that when they watch, they should look for the step pattern, detail of the hands and the energy and rhythm with which it was performed).

b) Show the remaining steps on the video extract (a series of different step patterns). In their groups of six, ask them to select four of the steps to use in creating their own section. The section must include unison, canon and a variety of group formations and pathways. Pupils should make decisions about:

- the order of the steps
- how many of each step they will perform (suggest two, four or eight of each)
- facing
- group pattern and pathways.
- timings.

### Task 6

**Advanced Bollywood Steps**

Able pupils can either create their own Bollywood-style steps or watch the video extract of Bollywood-style steps, in order to gain further ideas to incorporate in their own section.

Video Extract: Example Material – Advanced Bollywood Steps.

### Task 7

**Linking Bollywood Steps section with the taught material**

Each group should decide the order in which to perform their sections. It may be necessary to create a simple transition to link the sections together.

### Task 8

**Analysing the group formations and pathways**

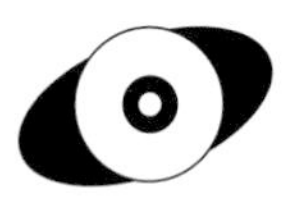

Pupil Worksheet: Analysis of Group Formations and Pathways.

Each group should analyse the formations and pathways within their dance so far. Ask the pupils to complete the analysis sheet by drawing and describing what they have done using key spatial and relationship words.

## Task 9

**Video observation: identifying the link between the lyrics and movement**

The purpose of this task is to illustrate one of the key features of Bollywood choreography: the dancers' physical interpretation of the lyrics and storyline of a song. The extract to be viewed contains subtitles that will assist pupils in making direct links between what they see, hear and the narrative being expressed.

a) Watch the opening dance scene from *Bride and Prejudice* again (at approx 5mins 35secs from the start of the film). Ask pupils to look for examples of movements that are directly related to the words being sung, for example:

- when the words 'you razor sharp girls' are sung, the male dancers perform a gesture with one hand that slices and cuts across the throat
- when the words 'can sting like a bee' are sung, the male dancers perform a short sharp stabbing gesture with the fingers of their right hand pressed together
- when the words 'as the stream flows *down the hill*' are sung, the female dancers shunt backwards on both feet with the arms seeping down from high to low, coming in towards the body.

b) Lead the whole group in discussion, ensuring pupils explain and show examples of movements that directly relate to the words.

## Task 10

**Creating a short phrase of movement that interprets the lyrics**

Ask the group to write a short narrative paragraph, which could be included in a Bollywood song, on which they will base their Bollywood actions. The paragraph should make reference to some of the key Bollywood film themes, such as love, hate, betrayal, anger and fear. It may be useful to include some of the following words:

| | |
|---|---|
| Shy | Strength |
| Searching | Surprise |
| Beating heart | Anger |
| Rejection | Talking |
| Beckoning | Laughing |
| Combing hair | Flying |
| Looking in the mirror | Stinging |
| Flower | Weeping |
| River | |

Not every single word of the paragraph needs an associated action, just those that help to tell the story.

## Task 11

**Linking all three sections of the dance together**

As pupils link all three sections of their dance together, provide time for them to rehearse their material.

## Task 12

**Performing the complete dance**

# Unit 3: Cog (Year 7)

## About the Unit

This unit focuses on the Honda Accord advert, *Cog*. The advert highlights precision in engineering and how the individual parts of a car come together, in an elaborate chain reaction, to make the car work. Pupils will explore ideas, such as how to create mechanical movement, and depict events that might occur on a typical daily car journey.

The unit focuses on coordination of isolated body parts, such as arms and legs, when on the spot and travelling. Interlocking with a partner and using physical manipulation to initiate actions that go up and down, around and around, and side to side is the main technical challenge within this unit.

Choreographically, pupils concentrate on spatial features, such as dimensional movement and contrasting pathways. Furthermore, the use of cause and effect helps build pupils' work from solo to duet and into small group work. The structure of the dance should reflect the structure of the advert; it progresses from individual car parts to how the parts connect and work together, culminating in a car journey, during which a number of events take place.

As they work, pupils identify and describe key actions and dynamic, spatial and relationship features of the advert. They also make connections between what they see in the advert with the movements they learn, create and perform.

This unit serves as a useful introduction to contact pair work. Before pupils can go on to do more advanced lifts and catches, taking full body weight, it is essential that they are comfortable and confident working in close proximity to and with other dancers. Within this unit there are opportunities to introduce basic contact work but within a relatively objective and functional context that requires little intimacy or emotion.

## Resources

**Music**

- 'Loops of Fury' by the Chemical Brothers on *Singles 93–03* (Astralwerks/Emd, 2003).
- 'Timber' by Coldcut and Hexstatic on *The Best Dance Album of All Time* (Muzik Magazine, 2002).
- 'Machines Are Us' by Faithless on *Outrospective* (Arista, 2001).
- 'Driving in My Car' by Madness on *The Business* (Virgin Records, 1993).

**Additional Resources and Information**

There are several alternative pieces of music you can use for this unit, such as:

- 'Chemical Beats' by The Chemical Brothers on *Singles 93–03*.
- 'Steam Machine' by Daft Punk on *Human After All* (Virgin Records, 2005).
- 'Kinesthesia' by Aphex Twin on *26 Mixes for Cash* (Warp Records, 2003).

For discussion on the advert, and more information visit: www.snopes.com/autos/business/hondacog.asp

and search on the internet using the key words, 'cog', 'Honda' and 'Telegraph'.

## Expectations

### Performance

- **Demonstrate precision and coordination within isolated gestures of the arms and legs, when on the spot and travelling** (eg pumping the arms up and down while stepping from side to side).
- **Demonstrate dynamic clarity in relation to different speeds and tensions** (eg slow, sustained pressing actions; sharp and quick cutting actions; swinging, circling and punching actions).
- **Demonstrate ways of initiating and responding to a partner's actions with control and accuracy** (eg interlocking with different body parts, initiating a partner to turn while managing the speed and energy).

### Composition

- **Create movements appropriate to the theme, with an emphasis on key spatial features** (eg various actions that go around and around, up and down, side to side and latch on, along various pathways and on the spot).
- **Develop movements using cause and effect to show a chain reaction** (eg use actions, such as nudge, press, pull and knock, to initiate movement between dancers in a logical sequence).
- **Create a short narrative, as a group, that depicts a journey's keys moments in an abstract way** (eg making an emergency stop and going over a speed bump).

### Appreciation

- **Identify key actions, and spatial, dynamic and relationship features of the advert** (eg describe what actions the various car parts do and how the knock-on effect progresses through the advert).
- **Recognise the link between the action, sound made and dynamic qualities of the movement** (eg how the thudding or whirring sounds reflect the heaviness or lightness of their movements).
- **Analyse and describe another group dance for pathways, directions and key narrative moments** (eg how the group travels forwards, reverses, negotiates corners and runs out of petrol).

## Cog

This unit builds on duet work to introduce working in quartets. The dance reflects the structure of the advert, looking at the way individual car parts interlink and then create a chain reaction to set the car in motion. Finally, as a group, pupils create their own eventful journey.

### Task 1

**Introducing the dance idea**

a) Provide a brief introduction to the Honda Accord advert, *Cog* and share the following information with the class:

- The advert took five months to plan and make, and required painstaking patience.
- Eighty-eight actual car parts were used in the making of the advert.
- No computer graphics or trick photography were used; only one special effect.
- It is a technically perfect chain reaction, intended to mirror the precision that has gone into the making of the car.

Video Extract: Honda Accord Advert.

b) Show the pupils the advert and ask them to consider the following questions:

- How many attempts did it take to film the advert?
  Answer: *606!*
- What is Honda's sales pitch? Why should you buy this car?
  Answer: *You should buy this car because Honda knows how to put cars together; Honda knows how to make cars that work. Closing statement: 'Isn't it nice when something just works?' The cars are based on precision in engineering.*
- What happens at the end of the advert?
  Answer: *The car rolls off the production line.*

c) Show the pupils that advert again and get them to list the parts of the car they recognise.

### Task 2

**Completing the advert analysis chart**

Together with the pupils, complete the advert analysis chart, identifying the action and the spatial, dynamic and relationship features of the advert.

Pupil Worksheet: *Cog* – Advert Analysis Chart.

Explain that some of the elements identified in the analysis chart will form the basis of the movement vocabulary for the dance. For example, emphasis will be placed on the concepts of 'around and around' (to reflect wheels) 'up and down' (to reflect pistons) 'side to side' (to reflect windscreen wipers) and movements that interlock (to reflect cogs). The structure of the advert will be reflected in the final dance where, for example, individual parts join together to work as a whole.

### Task 3

**Introducing the movement vocabulary**

Pupils learn examples of short movement phrases to introduce the concept of going around and around. The purpose of these examples is to introduce the appropriate style of movement and to provide pupils with some vocabulary they can use alongside their own ideas.

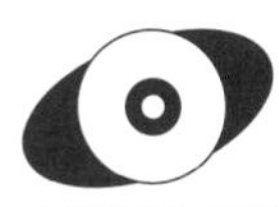

Video Extract: Example Material – Introductory Actions.

**The impact of language**

The choice of language and the use of voice can have a significant effect on the quality of the pupils work (ie the dynamics and precision they show in performance and the range of movements they create). For example, the word 'walk' could result in a plain and uninteresting stepping action. In contrast, the words 'stride', 'plod', 'scurry', 'march' or 'stomp' result in movements that communicate different expressive outcomes.

The use of onomatopoeic words (words that sound like the action/meaning they communicate, such as 'slice') is particularly helpful.

### Task 4

**Creating a solo phrase: individual car parts that go around and around**

By the end of the task, each pupil will have created a short solo phrase, based on material selected from the guided improvisation. This phrase should:

- be performed mainly on the spot
- include a mix of isolated body actions and whole body actions
- show a range of dynamics identified on the advert analysis chart.

a) Ask pupils to select one action from Task 3 that goes around and around to repeatedly perform on the spot.

b) Select three pupils that show contrasting examples of actions that go around and around and highlight the key differences between them. (For example, one pupil might demonstrate around and around with an individual body part, another through an action with the whole body, and one at floor level.)

c) Ask pupils to perform a different action, taking on board the examples shared. On your command, they must instantly swap to another action. Repeat this process about six times, providing prompts for the pupils; for example, encouraging pupils to use unusual body parts, such as knees and elbows, and different levels.

d) Ask the pupils to now select from their improvisation to create a short solo phrase that illustrates contrasting ways of going around and around.

e) Once the actions have been selected, ordered and practiced, provide a list of dynamic words taken from the Advert Analysis Chart worksheet (eg quickly, smoothly, slowly, judderingly).

f) Encourage the pupils to apply these dynamic qualities to actions within their solo dance.

g) Allow time to practise and refine.

h) Organise half the class to watch the other half while they perform. Ask the audience to identify unusual examples of ways to show the action of 'around and around'.

**Guiding pupils through improvisation**

Helping pupils create their own material can be one of the most exciting experiences for the teacher, as pupils may amaze you with their imaginative ideas. The process is a balance between providing enough structure (without enforcing your own ideas) to ensure pupils feel secure and stay on task, compared with too much freedom, or tasks that are so open-ended, which can leave children not knowing where to start.

Improvisation tasks should be kept relatively short and tightly structured. You need to build, progressively, on small, achievable physical challenges. In order to promote divergent and original responses, you should use communication designed to engage pupils thinking (eg prompt questions such as, 'what might happen if...?' or 'can you find another way to...?' as opposed to 'try this!')

### Task 5

**Learning a set phrase: individual car parts that go up and down and side to side**

In order to further extend pupils' movement vocabulary and offer a contrast of teaching approaches, pupils now learn the set phrase. The phrase includes movements that go up and down and from side to side, depicting actions, such as dropping, plummeting, nudging, springing and catapulting.

Video Extract: Set Material – Car Parts Phrase.

### Task 6

**Combining the taught material with their solo phrase to create an extended phrase**

Ensure the pupils decide the order and complexity of the extended phrase, either:

- the taught 'up and down', 'side to side' phrase followed by their own 'around' phrase
- their own 'around' phrase followed by the taught 'up and down', 'side to side' phrase
- a new phrase that switches from one of the previous phrases to the other.

### Task 7

**Transition: travel to a partner**

Demonstrate how an action taken from the extended phrase (performed primarily on the spot) can be developed into a travelling phrase (eg how a single arm rotation can be performed while stepping and turning). Pupils should then create their own transition to their partner.

### Task 8

**Interlocking with a partner: creating a cause-and-effect duet**

The imagery behind this section of the dance is how a cog (a toothed wheel) latches on and interlocks with another cog to initiate movement (cause and effect).

By the end of the task, each pair will have created a short duet. This duet should:

- show a variety of ways to hook onto a partner and make a partner move up and down, around and around and side to side
- show a range of dynamics identified on the Advert Analysis Chart.

a) Ask pupils to view examples of how to interlock with a partner and initiate movement.

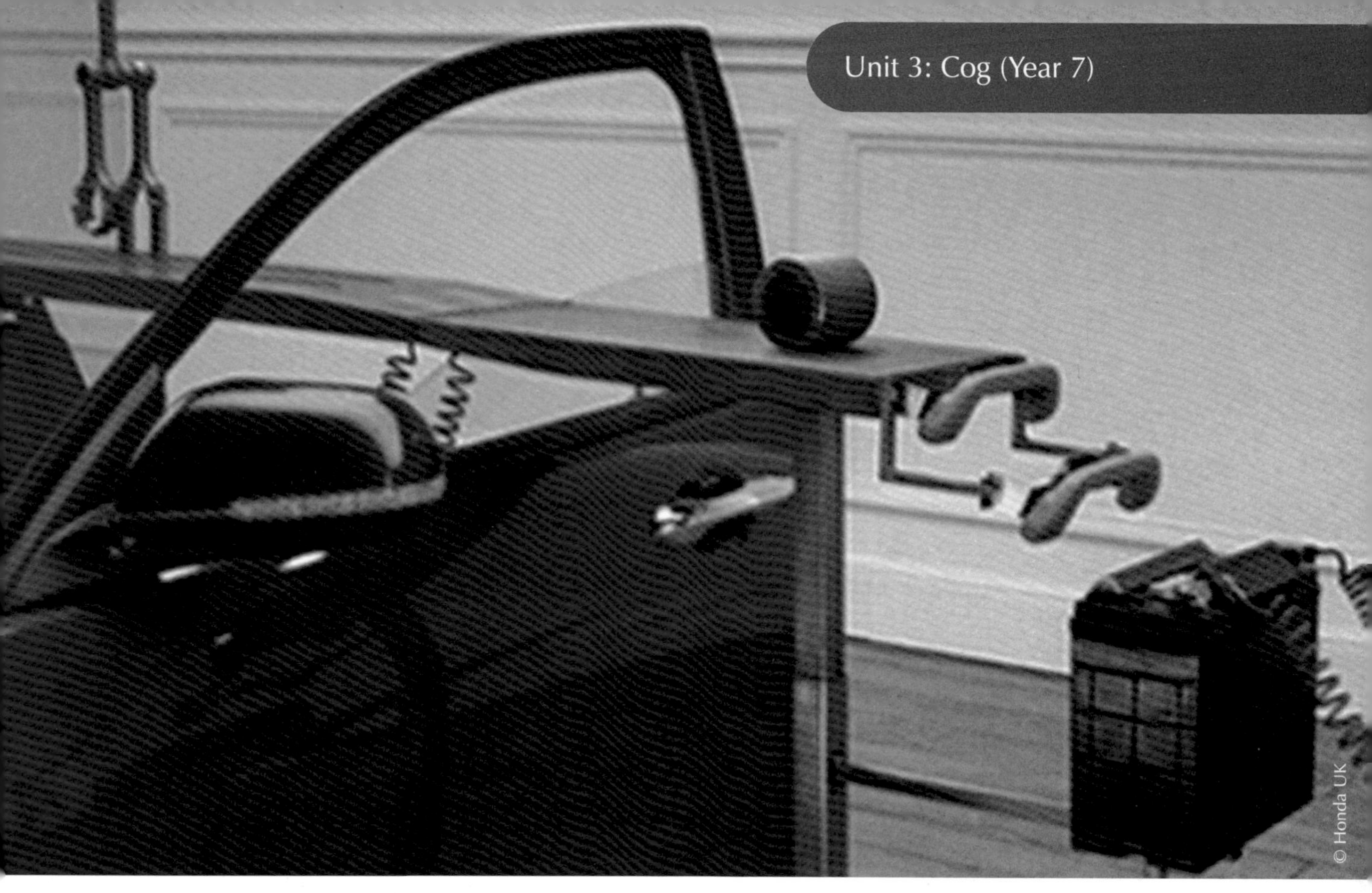

Video Extract: Example Material – Interlocking Movement.

b) Ask pupils to complete the following movement pattern:
   - Pupil A holds a static shape taken from their extended phrase.
   - Pupil B latches on and initiates movement.
   - Pupils swap roles and repeat process.
   - Pupils continue to repeat this process, exploring different static shapes and latches.

c) Ask pupils to select their best ideas and build them into a phrase.

d) Ask pupils to link all sections of the dance so far. So: extended phrase, transition (travel to partner) and interlocking phrase.

### Task 9

**Transition: pairs travel to another pair, to finish in a horizontal line**

In a similar process to Task 7, take an aspect of the dance so far and develop it using travelling, this time with a partner.

### Task 10

**Interlocking in a small group: creating a chain reaction**

Having explored the concept of interlocking and initiating movement, pupils can now be challenged to develop this idea further by working in groups of four.

Pupils create a phrase of movement which progresses up and down the line. The phrase is to finish in a square block of four (for instance, representing four passengers in a car: two in the front and two in the back). As pupils work, remind them to think about the use of different dynamics, various levels/heights and interesting ways to latch on and interlock.

### Task 11

**Reinforcing the importance of dynamics – dynamic analysis of *Cog***

Show pupils the advert, *Cog*, again and, together, with the pupils, create a list of words that describe the sounds. For example:

- thud
- thwack
- plop
- scrape
- catapult
- boing
- whirr
- creak
- crash
- ding
- glug.

Discuss with the pupils how the sounds help emphasise the actions being performed. Make a link with the sounds described and the contrasting dynamics pupils are endeavouring to show.

## Task 12

**Learning a series of basic step patterns that travel around the space**

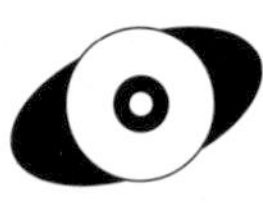

Video Extract: Example Material – Travelling Step Patterns.

## Task 13

**The journey**

The image for this section is one where the car has now been purchased and is taken from the production line and used on daily journeys.

a) Ask pupils to describe their daily journey to school, identifying key manoeuvres of the vehicle (eg reversing, three-point turns, roundabouts and overtaking).

b) Remaining in the formation of the square block of four formed at the end of Task 10 (to reflect people sitting in front and back seats of a car), ask pupils to create a short journey, using the material learnt in Task 12, to show a variety of car manoeuvres in an abstract way.

c) As pupils work, additional ideas can be added. For example:
- stalling
- changing gear
- making an emergency stop
- going over speed bumps
- running out of petrol
- driving up a steep hill.

## Task 14

**Refining and performing the complete dance to the whole class**

## Task 15

**Performing and observing**

Pupils draw the pathway of the journey and describe it using key spatial terms for the pathways and direction changes, noting particular events that happen en route.

# Unit 4: Guernica (Year 8)

## About the Unit

This unit takes its inspiration from the painting *Guernica* (1937) by Pablo Picasso. The unit makes cross-curricular links with art and history and shows pupils how other art forms and historic events can be a powerful stimuli for dance.

The unit focuses on an emotive, moral issue. The pupils analyse and interpret the painting, using both the visual imagery of the shapes and a discussion of events that inspired the artist.

A key focus of this unit is the development of expressive skills. Pupils are asked to empathise with the people of Guernica and portray images, such as chaos, pain, outrage and brutality, within their own dances. The use of focus and facial expression, contracting, twisting and arching the spine and forming geometric shapes with the body, aid the powerful and vivid expression of the work.

Choreographically, pupils will reflect the composition of the painting, using devices such as overlapping and changes of level to represent the work. The dance progresses from duet to small-group work.

As they work, pupils should make connections between their movements, body shapes and expressions and the content and meaning of the painting.

Do not be put off by the choice of painting. Young people are surprisingly able to deal with complex works of art. They identify obvious features and create their own interpretations about the people and events depicted. Allowing pupils to suggest their own interpretation of the work is valuable, however, assisting them to gain a deeper understanding and an insight into the artist's intention will impact on the integrity of their dancing. In order to do this, you need to undertake research about the painting and the events that inspired it. This unit would create an opportunity to make cross-curricular links with art and history.

## Resources

**Music**

- 'O Fortuna' from *Carmina Burana* by Carl Orff (most classical versions are suitable).
- 'Evacuation' on *The Killing Fields* (Virgin Records, 1992) soundtrack.
- 'New World' and 'Intensive Time' by Philip Glass on *Naqoyqatsi (Life as War)* (Sony, 2002).

**Painting**

- Photos of the painting are easily available. Search the Internet for Picasso's Guernica.

**Additional Resources and Information**

There are many websites where you can access images of the painting, along with historical facts, information and suggested interpretations of key images. Here are a few:

http://en.wikipedia.org/wiki/Guernica_(painting)

http://www.deakin.edu.au/education/visarts/example1.htm

http://www.spanish-fiestas.com/art/picasso-guernica.htm

http://www.answers.com/topic/guernica-painting

## Expectations

### Performance

- **Demonstrate clarity and expressive use of the spine when performing** (eg twisting, arching and contracting positions are taken to their extreme).
- **Demonstrate good technique when jumping, falling and rolling at speed** (eg take-off and landings show control and clarity of shape in the air; flight actions have an 'explosive' quality, showing power and vitality; falling and rolling actions use the floor safely).
- **Demonstrate appropriate facial expression/characterisation showing emotion** (eg open mouths as if screaming, eyes wide-open as if terrified).

### Composition

- **Create movements that reflect key shapes, images and emotions within the painting** (eg out-stretched hands and upward focus, use of torso [twisted, arched, contracted] when creating key shapes and phrases of movement).
- **Compose various *tableaux* in small groups that reflect the compositional structure of the painting** (eg the use of over-lapping and contrasting levels to show the chaos and juxtaposition of body parts).
- **Create a dance based on a given narrative** (eg a dance to show the bomb being dropped and the response to this).

### Appreciation

- **Identify and interpret what is seen in the painting, offering explanations for responses** (eg describe key motifs and point to objective features of the work to support answers).
- **Discuss the moral issues surrounding the events depicted in the painting and how this is shown in the dance** (eg describe how the fleeing woman in the painting might feel).
- **Evaluate the success of other groups in communicating the dance idea** (eg success at depicting chaos, pain and outrage).

## Guernica

This unit builds from solo work into developing work as quartets. The final dance follows a narrative structure based around events that happened in Guernica. The dance concludes with tableaux images that resemble key aspects of the painting.

### Task 1

**Introducing the dance idea**

a) Give each pair a copy of the painting *Guernica* by Picasso.

Ask each pair to discuss their responses to the key question:

*What do you think the painting is about and why do you think this?*

b) Facilitate the sharing of answers. Pupils should identify what the painting is about and support their answer by pointing to specific features of the painting.

### Task 2

**Teacher-led short discussion about the bombing of Guernica and key motifs in the painting**

The purpose of this discussion is to set the scene for the unit and to give pupils some information about the event and the painting. In addition, it is hoped that this information will begin to generate discussion around the horror and injustice inflicted on the people of Guernica. Pupils should be asked to empathise with the event and engage with their own emotions, imagining how they would respond in such a situation.

Teacher Prompt Sheet: Historic Facts About the Bombing of Guernica.

**Dealing with sensitive topics**

Dance provides the ideal opportunity for the discussion of sensitive and controversial matters. When dealing with issues from another time or place, it often helps if you make parallels with current events around the world. When drawing parallels and opening up discussion, you need to be very aware of the difference between empathy and first-hand experience, and to use your professional judgement in selecting tasks. On these occasions, returning back to focus directly on the painting should alleviate anxiety. Making these connections typically helps to motivate and inspire pupils.

### Task 3

**Six key positions**

Ask pupils to copy the six positions illustrated on the worksheets. As pupils learn the positions, attention should be given to making links between the actions being performed and the imagery and factual content discussed previously. The following should be highlighted:

- How the spine twists, arches and contracts.
- The repeated use of outstretched hands and wide-spread fingers.
- The use of facial expression (eg open mouths, wide eyes and upward focus).

Pupil Worksheet: *Guernica* – Key Positions.

### Task 4

**Linking the six positions into a phrase**

Video Extract: Example Material – Linking Shapes Together.

a) Demonstrate, or view the extract, to see how the shapes can be linked together, focusing on ways to move into and out of the positions, showing different dynamic qualities.

b) Using the worksheet from Task 2 to help their memory, get pupils decide on an order for the positions and then ask them to create their own phrase of movement.

### Task 5

**Reciprocal task**

In pairs, ask pupils to watch their partner's phrase and comment on the following:

- Do they look as if they are stretching beyond their fingers and toes?
- Can they see all six shapes clearly with a mixture of twists, arches and contractions?
- Are they using their focus and facial expressions to add meaning to the actions?
- Can they remember the phrase from beginning to end?

Pupils should be encouraged to give positive, constructive feedback with clear targets for improvement. Time should then be given for the corrections to be worked on and then reviewed again by the same observer for signs of improvement.

## Task 6

**Learning travelling phrases from you or direct from the video extract**

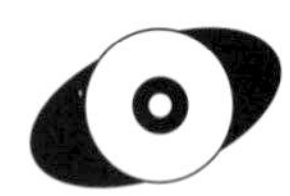

Video Extract: Example Material – Travelling Phrases.

a) zigzag pathway with asymmetrical leaps

b) stepping, rolling and turning

c) low-level travelling

## Task 7

**Linking solo phrases with travelling phrases into a given narrative structure**

Divide the pupils into groups of four.

Each pupil now has their own solo phrase, which includes the six positions. Common to the group of four are the three taught travelling phrases. The group are now ready to start structuring the material to form Section 1 of their dance. The narrative dictates the overall structure of the dance; however, there are numerous opportunities for the group to make their own choreographic choices within this.

**Section 1 – Narrative structure**

- **Bombs begin dropping on Guernica**

  Direct the dancers to decide whether to start on or off the imaginary stage space. Each dancer should choose one of the three taught travelling phrases to perform frantically around the space.

  Ask all dancers to freeze in a protective huddle in a small space on stage.

  **Choreographic prompts to give pupils:**

  – Remind pupils of the need to choreograph their pathways. Although the intention is that it looks chaotic, this must be tightly rehearsed to avoid accidents, with pupils clearly knowing their own pathways. Prompt pupils to use zigzags and haphazard pathways to depict the chaos.

  – The groups need to make decisions about the opening travelling section (eg will all dancers perform the same phrase repeatedly, or will all three travelling phrases be seen in the opening section?).

- **Group watches in horror and then, together, flees for cover**

  From the freeze position, the group looks slowly to the sky and follows the pathway of an imaginary fighter plane until it goes over their head, tipping them off balance.

  Dancers flee together to a new 'safe space' on stage where they form a different huddle.

  **Choreographic prompts to give pupils:**

  – Suggest that the huddle is on different levels and that pupils need to consider the importance of facial expression (eg wide-eyed and open-mouthed like the unheard scream).

  – Groups need to select, from the examples taught in Task 6, another way to travel to the new space.

- **Another bomb drops and individuals flee**

  From the new huddle, the dancers break away in canon. Choosing their own travelling phrase, they finish and spread out in the space.

  **Choreographic prompts to give pupils:**

  – Suggest that the canon has a clear and simple structure (eg an equal four-count delay).

  – Explain to dancers that they may need to adapt their travelling phrase to a new direction, in order to finish with the group spread out.

- **A focus on individuals**

  Simultaneously, each dancer performs their solo phrase, which includes the six positions.

**Choreographic prompts to give pupils:**

- Emphasise the importance of dynamic contrasts within each individual's phrase.
- Suggest that each dancer faces a different direction to start.
- Return to reinforce the performance qualities outlined in Task 3.

**The importance of dynamics**

You can never over-estimate the significance of dynamics when choreographing and performing. Pupils need to be constantly reminded of the relevance of the dynamics in relation to the dance idea. Using a rich descriptive dynamic vocabulary, along with the use of visual imagery, can greatly influence pupils' performance.

## Task 8

### Section 2 – Creating tableaux

a) Within the group, each dancer must select a different key image from the painting and create a position that reflects it.

b) Using the four positions, the group then explores ways to overlap their individual images, creating their own painting. Dancers experiment with being in front or behind each other, keeping in side profile to maintain the two-dimensional imagery in the painting.

Repeat the process in step a) three more times, until each dancer has four different positions. The group then constructs three more tableaux images and finds short, logical transitions between them.

Discuss with pupils how the use of overlapping as a choreographic device reflects the sense of overlapping in the painting.

## Task 9

### Refining and performing the complete dance

a) Ask pupils to link Sections 1 and 2 together. Provide time for them to rehearse their material.

b) Read and discuss the extract (see worksheet) from Picasso's poem *Franco's Dream and Lie* to reinforce an understanding of the pain and suffering experienced. Discuss the importance of clarifying the dynamic content of the choreography and how it helps communicate the dance idea. This poem was written to accompany a series of etchings entitled *Franco's Dream and Lie*, which also depicts aspects of the Spanish Civil War.

Pupil Worksheet: Franco's Dream and Lie.

c) Provide time for final refinement of dances and then get the groups to share their work with the class.

## About the Unit

This unit takes as its starting point a collage of images related to living in an urban environment. The unit taps into aspects of youth culture, such as popular music, street dance and Parkour. Consideration is also given to exploring the ways in which people fight for and share space in crowded situations, and to the energy and intensity of city life.

This unit focuses on the basic techniques of street dancing and travelling using Parkour-style movements, and the challenges of working with other dancers in a restricted space.

Choreographically, pupils explore and solve physical problems related to overcrowding in small spaces. They also devise phrases of movement that reflect the way Parkourists move around cities, travelling over, through, around and between buildings and obstacles. Finally, pupils create and structure movements in a street-dance style.

As they work, pupils analyse basic action, spatial, dynamic and relationship components of Parkour and street dance.

Tapping into popular culture is a great way to engage pupils. However, this unit attempts to go deeper than simply providing pupils with the instant appeal of replicating 'moves' they have seen on their favourite pop video. Whilst having the opportunity to do this is integral to the unit, it can also be quite restricting. Therefore, embracing street dance within the context of wider urban issues opens up opportunities for work of a broader creative nature.

When working in a street-dance style it is important to be aware of the sexually explicit nature and inappropriate language expressed in some of the music and movement. As the teacher, you will need to censor pupils' movements and your choice of music to ensure its suitability for young people.

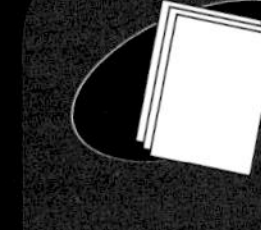

## Resources

### Music

- 'Break and enter' from *Music for the Jilted Generation* by The Prodigy (Mute U.S., 1995).
- 'Expander' on *Accelerator* (Cleopatra, 1996) by Future Sounds of London.
- 'Hey Boy, Hey Girl' on *Surrender* (Astralwerks, 1999) by The Chemical Brothers.
- 'Planet Rock' on The Real Old School Revival *Electro Breakdance: Vol (1)* (Telstar, 2002). Most Hip Hop/break dance tracks would be a suitable alternative. NB: Some tracks will carry parental guidance stickers.

### Video/DVD

- *Jump Britain* (Carbon Princess, 2005) and *Jump London* (directed by Mike Christie, Carbon Media, 2004) DVDs.
- *You Got Served* (Sony Pictures, 2005).

For photo images of crowded underground scenes, search Google Images for: 'London Underground rush hour', 'tube in rush hour' and 'crowded tube'.

### Additional Resources and Information

For images, discussion and video footage of tracuers, go to:

- www.parkour.com
- www.rousette.org.uk/blog/archives/2003/09/11/free-running
- www.urbanfreeflow.com
- www.worldwidewords.org/turnsofphrase/tp-fre1.htm
- http://en.wikipedia.org/wiki/Street_dance (or Hip_hop_dance)

## Expectations

### Performance

- **Demonstrate confidence, energy and an appropriate attitude when performing in a street-dance style** (eg flamboyant gestures and poses, a clear contrast of dynamics between popping, locking and breaking movements – see the Glossary for definitions of these movements).
- **Demonstrate rhythmic accuracy when performing step patterns with complex timing and accents** (eg moving on and off the beat precisely, moving in time with different pieces of music and showing a sense of rhythm in the whole body).
- **Demonstrate control and elegance when performing acrobatic movements alone and with a partner** (eg control when landing from a height and clarity of shape when moving over and around other dancers).

### Composition

- **Respond imaginatively to improvisation tasks, based on key concepts related to the dance idea** (eg unusual ways to portray claiming space on a crowded tube, interacting with other people in tight spaces and Parkour-like journeys that move over, through and around).
- **Create/select movements in a street-dance style** (eg various ways of locking, popping and breaking).
- **Structure movements into a routine that reflects aspects of street dance choreography viewed on video** (eg how dances move from solos to group work, 'tagging in' for transitions, and the use of different numerical variations).

### Appreciation

- **View pictures and videos and describe key action, spatial, dynamic and relationship features** (eg the spatial relationship depicted in the photos showing the overcrowded underground, the actions of the traceurs as they move around the city and the dynamics of the street dancers).
- **Comment on the views and opinions expressed by leading professionals in Parkour and street dance** (eg make suggestions about how Sebastien Foucan's philosophy on Parkour relates to daily living).

## Urban

This unit culminates in a group dance made up of three sections. While the sections are distinct from one another, they relate to the common overarching theme of urban living. Short transitions should be included to link the sections together to form a complete dance. Below is a summary of the main images of each section.

**Section 1 – Fighting for space**

Main images:

- People entering the London Underground from all directions, going through the turnstile and then boarding a crowded tube.
- Passengers struggling to find space; individuals attempting to move through the crowded carriage.
- People filing off the tube and exiting the underground, feeling the need to move more freely.

**Section 2 – The urban playground**

Main images:

- Participants in Parkour (traceurs) treat the urban landscape as a playground. They use man-made structures as an obstacle course to go over, under, around and through. A group of traceurs share a common pathway.
- They move around the city, jumping gaps between buildings, swinging around posts and vaulting obstacles en route.

**Section 3 – Street dance**

Main image: Hip-hop style choreographed routines, battles and free-styling.

## Section 1 – Fighting for space

### Task 1

**Introducing the dance idea**

Search Google Images for downloadable pictures of the London Underground to show pupils. In particular, select images that show lots of people getting on and off the trains, people in crowded carriages and people funnelling into smaller spaces (eg entering the tube station, going through the tube door and filing onto the escalator).

Search under the headings:

- London Underground rush hour
- Tube in rush hour
- Crowded tube.

a) Show pupils different images of crowds on the London underground.

b) Facilitate a discussion about the experiences of the people in the pictures. For example, ask the pupils to:

- describe what is happening in the picture
- consider the people in the picture (eg if they could tell you what they were thinking and how they were feeling, what would they say?)
- describe some of the key spatial relationships they see in the picture (eg people are very close to one another; they go from a crowd into a single file).

### Task 2

**Creating Section 1 – Fighting for space**

The whole class will have a common framework for this section of the dance. However, individuals and groups should be encouraged to make personal interpretations in response to the task.

Split the class into groups of six dancers. Each group needs a rectangular box marked out on the floor to represent a carriage on a tube. The corners should be marked using gaffer/masking tape.

Guide each group simultaneously through the improvisation framework below, encouraging pupils to explore, before selecting and structuring the section. For each task, pupils need time to find a number of different answers, before deciding on the final movements to be performed.

a) Passengers start away from the marked-out area and stand randomly in the space, facing different directions.

b) Passengers hurry towards an imaginary turnstile, in front of, but some distance from the tube carriage. Each group member, in rapid succession, passes through the turnstile and performs a turning action of their choice (eg a spin or jump-turn).

c) Passengers travel towards the tube and each dancer selects a way of getting onto the tube; for example, they:

- squeeze through a small gap in the door
- jump onto the tube just before the doors close
- push a way into the carriage, using the side of their body and their shoulder.

Pupils should be encouraged to make their movements dance-like by exaggerating, elaborating, repeating and/or varying their actions, rather than just using representational, mime-like actions. Pupils should think about creating phrases rather than single movements.

d) Pupils create a short section of movement, based on the image of claiming space on a crowded tube. The improvisation that follows is built around two key concepts:

- squeezing through tight spaces
- interacting with other people in tight spaces.

Pupils explore each concept and, as they do, the complexity of the improvisation builds. The improvisation is designed to give pupils physical problems to solve that relate to the idea, as opposed to asking for representational, mime-like actions, such as standing with one arm in the air, pretending to hold an underground strap. It is, of course, acceptable for pupils to use such an iconic image momentarily in their dance; however, the aim is to explore other ways in which the crowded tube scenario can be portrayed.

Passengers stand close together (facing different directions) but with enough space to move between one another.

## Squeezing through tight spaces

In turn, each passenger finds a pathway that they can squeeze through and around, and past passengers. As they squeeze through, pupils should think about leading with different body parts, such as their elbow, hip, heel or arm. As the improvisation builds, some of the following ideas may be included:

- starting to squeeze through a space in one direction and then seeing a bigger space somewhere else and going for it
- squeezing past different passengers in quick succession
- squeezing past and stepping over imaginary luggage
- more than one person in the carriage squeezing through at the same time.

Challenge pupils to create movement that is different to that of the previous person.

## Interacting with other people in tight spaces

The squeezing idea develops to include the use of other people to lean on, push off, assist or pull against. Some of the following ideas might be included:

- pulling against one or two passengers' shoulders to leaver through into a space
- knocking into one person, which sets up a brief chain reaction, jostling everyone into a new position.

e) Having explored a variety of ideas, now ask the pupils to select from the improvisation and set a short section that shows various ways of `fighting for space'. As they set their dance, pupils should take account of the music and aim to set their movements to the phrasing of the music.

f) Pupils invent a scenario to include within their section. For example:

- two passengers go for the same space at the same time
- an incident occurs at one end of the carriage, sending all the passengers rushing down to the other end
- an emergency stop and power cut happens, which freezes the movement temporarily.

g) The section ends with passengers exiting through the tube doors and funnelling their way through the busy turnstiles, out onto the street. Refer to part (b) of this section for ideas.

**Moving beyond the obvious**

When working creatively, your main challenge is helping pupils to think beyond the first, most obvious answer. Working in this way is about getting the pupils to think divergently. Pupils must understand that the object of the exercise is to find different responses to the same task, and that this can only be achieved through trial and error. An inevitable consequence of trial and error is that not all the material created will be used in the final dance; some of it will be inappropriate for communicating the dance idea and therefore discarded. In choreography, there is no right or wrong answer; it is just a matter of appropriateness.

While some pupils whole-heartedly embrace the opportunity to create their own material, others find this process frustrating and claim they have no ideas. Some are self-conscious or reluctant to explore an idea further than their first, most obvious response ('I've done that, Miss', 'Sir, what's next?'). These first responses are neither interesting, unusual or challenging to the pupils' thinking.

In order to achieve greater originality, you need to be brave enough to watch pupils struggle as they search for different answers to the task and be ready to challenge the pupils who are satisfied, all too quickly, with their first, most obvious response. While a certain amount of struggle is an inevitable part of discovery, there are strategies that the teacher can use when setting composition tasks and assisting the pupils as they work. These will reduce anxiety and maximise the creative output. A good strategy is to either give the pupils a verbal example, or a practical demonstration. By doing this, the teacher will help pupils recognise the potential for different responses. Highlighting the more unusual movements created by pupils and sharing them with the class, will also provide the teacher with plenty of opportunity to praise and encourage those who have gone beyond the obvious response and to inspire others.

Where exploration is the priority, do not feel the pressure to set and show work. It is not essential that pupils have a finished product at the end of every lesson. Pressure to do this often dampens pupils' 'spirit of adventure' and willingness to try new ideas.

## Section 2 – The Urban playground

### Task 3

**Section 2 – Moving around an urban playground**

a) Provide brief information about the sport of Parkour. Give just enough information to help pupils understand the basics of the sport and to get them excited about the challenges ahead. Much of the information on the Teacher Prompt Sheet works best when integrated into practical work or when doing video observation, as in Tasks 4 and 5.

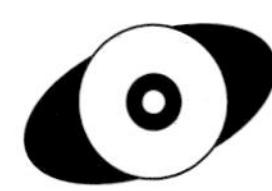

Teacher Prompt Sheet: Interesting Facts about Parkour.

### Task 4

**Learning set material – Parkour travelling phrase**

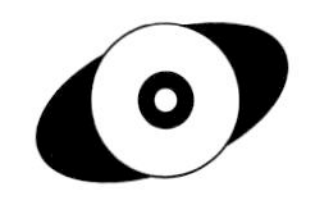

Video Extract: Set Material – Parkour Travelling Phrase.

When performing the travelling phrase, particular attention should be given to:

- soft, resilient landings when jumping from a height
- a sense of ongoing movement, punctuated by moments of stillness in balance
- safety aspects when taking weight on hands, such as the importance of placing hands flat on the floor and the need for body tension, strength and stability in the shoulders.

### Task 5

**Developing the set material**

In groups, pupils should decide their:

- timing (unison or canon)
- spatial relationships (two rows of three, three rows of two, follow the leader in single file etc).

## Task 6

**Video observation and analysis of *Jump Britain***

Show pupils extract(s) of Parkour from the video, *Jump Britain*. As they watch, ensure the pupils prepare to answer the following questions:

- What movements do you see performed (eg run, hop, leap, jump, spring, leaver, swing, balance and roll)?
- How do they tackle the obstacles (eg run along them, jump over them, circle around them and swing through them)?
- What are the physical and mental attributes that a traceur needs to stay safe (eg strength, flexibility, agility, balance, concentration, courage and good jumping and landing techniques)?

## Task 7

**Creating a travelling phrase that represents the ways in which traceurs move around the urban landscape**

Using the pupil worksheet, Moving Around an Urban Landscape, ask each group to create a short travelling phrase, selecting key images from the worksheet as the starting point.

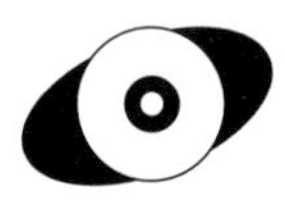

Pupil Worksheet: Moving Around an Urban Landscape.

## Task 8

**Linking the taught phrase with their own travelling phrase**

As a group, ensure pupils decide in which order to perform their material. Either the taught material followed by the travelling phrase or the travelling phrase followed by the taught material.

## Task 9

**Creating a short phrase of movement that uses a partner as an obstacle**

a) Lead a brief discussion about the nature of the work and how a partner is to be used to represent an obstacle to negotiate. Show examples from the video and then, using the first example on the DVD, select two pupils to demonstrate how to use a partner as an obstacle safely, and highlight the following key safety points:

- Take responsibility for your partner (let them know what they are going to attempt. Do not try anything that will put either one of you at risk).
- The need for a stable base (use of core stability) so that the person negotiating the obstacle feels safe and has a firm surface on which to support themselves.
- The need to know where weight can/cannot be placed (eg weight should not be placed in the small of the back).

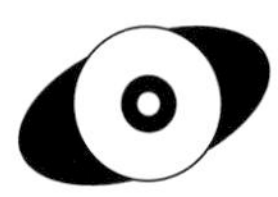

Video Extract: Set Material – Pair Obstacle Work.

b) Ask pupils to attempt the taught example in pairs to ensure that they understand the key safety principles. The pairs swap roles so that pupil A goes over pupil B, B over A and then A over B again.

c) Using the same base position, encourage pupils to begin to explore other options, such as:

- using one hand and then two hands
- jumping over one another without touching
- using the base to support a slow controlled balance
- as they gain in confidence and skill, beginning to vary the shape and height of base positions (initially starting with shapes that are low to the ground and easy to negotiate, then gradually getting higher and creating more interesting shapes with their bodies).

Periodically stop the class to share good examples.

d) Ask pupils to select and set at least three different examples of using a partner as an obstacle to build into a phrase, that travels around the space.

e) Ask pupils to combine all the material of Section 2 together (eg the taught material with spatial and timing developments, the created travelling phrase based on the worksheet and the obstacle phrase).

f) Transition – at the end of Section 2, pupils should create a 'photographic' image of a group of street dancers striking a pose.

### Task 10

**Joining Section 1 and Section 2 together**

### Task 11

**Discussing the quotation below**

*Parkour is unlike other extreme activities as it has a philosophy behind it.*

*Life is made of obstacles and challenges...to overcome them is to progress. If you become skilled at Parkour you gain something for the rest of your life.*

Sebastien Foucan, www.parkour.com

Ask pupils to read the quotation. Facilitate discussion based on the following questions:

- What challenges might Sebastien Foucan face when participating in Parkour (eg overcoming fear of failure, extreme physical challenges with the potential of injury and even death if the moves go wrong, and the challenge of being strong enough)?
- If he overcomes these challenges, how might it help him to overcome other challenges in his daily life (eg he will be more confident, self-assured and ready to face difficult situations; he will know that he can succeed and confront his fears)?

Ask pupils to consider incidences in their lives when they have faced their fears and then felt a sense of achievement when they have succeeded.

## Section 3 – Street dance

### Task 12

**Video observation: street dance**

Video Extract: Example Material – Brooke Milliner and Kemal Dempster.

a) Show pupils a short video extract of Brooke Milliner and Kemal Dempster 'freestyling'.

b) Together with the pupils, summarise key stylistic features of performance and choreography (eg popping, locking and breaking).

### Task 13

**Learning street-style movements**

There are a series of movements demonstrated on the video that the teacher can select from, in order to teach the pupils. Alternatively, pupils can copy the movements from the video themselves by watching them on a large screen, with the teacher directing the pace, number of repetitions and number of steps to be attempted.

A variety of actions from the categories of locking, popping and acrobatics should be taught.

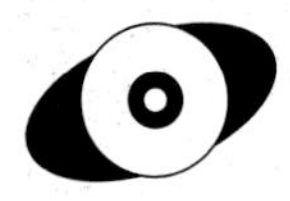

Video Extract: Example Material – Sheet-style Movements.

### Task 14

**Creating a street dance routine using the movements from Task 13**

a) Show pupils the extracts of short routines to exemplify how the movements can be seamlessly linked.

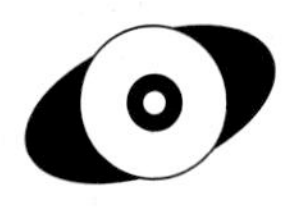

Video extract: Example Material – Street-dance Routines.

b) Give pupils time to create their own street dance routine using the movements learnt in Task 13, plus any additional street-style material. Additional material may come from movements they have seen on film, movements they know already or movements they create themselves. The routine should:

- include material from different categories within street dancing
- reflect the timing and energy of the music
- be performed with confidence and a 'street-style attitude'.

### Task 15

**Video observation**

Show the pupils the final dance scene from the film *You Got Served* (found approx one hour, 17 minutes and 40 seconds in) to identify features of good performance and to pick up any additional ideas they may wish to include within their own dance. The scene shows street dancers performing against one another in a high-level competition. As pupils watch, they are asked to look out for:

- the rhythmic accuracy of the dancers
- the flamboyancy and confidence of the dancers
- how each group has a distinct style and way of performing
- how the dancers 'tag one another in'
- how the dancers move from solos (where individuals get to show off their latest moves) to group work (where dancers perform in tight unison).

Facilitate discussion and summarise key points.

### Task 16

**Refining and making final additions/ amendments to Section 3**

Give pupils sufficient time to refine and develop their dance and decide how to personalise it.

### Task 17

**Linking Sections 1, 2 and 3 together and rehearsing, ready for performance**

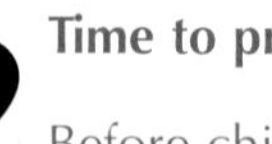

**Time to practise and refine**

Before children can perform with confidence, even to their peers, they need to know the material well. If they are worrying about what comes next, the quality of performance is likely to be neglected. Throughout each lesson, sufficient time must be given to allow pupils to consolidate their learning. Do not wait until the end of the unit. Repetition of phrases of movement will help consolidate new motor patterns; however, this does not constitute refining. Only once the new motor patterns have been learned, are pupils ready to start refining and concentrating on the detail of the movement (for example, the dynamic quality, use of focus and accuracy of timing).

Rehearsing material and 'picking' at the detail of it to improve clarity and precision is essential for high-quality work; however, some pupils find refining an exasperating and wearisome process. All pupils, therefore, require feedback to identify aspects for further improvement, in order to stay focused.

# Unit 6: Coliseum (Year 8)

## About the Unit

This unit takes classic images of gladiators as its inspiration. Scenes from films, such as *Spartacus* and *Gladiator*, provide visual stimuli and information about the life and work of the gladiator. In this unit, pupils will explore the personal traits needed to be a successful gladiator, their rigorous training regime and the brutal battles they fought inside the coliseum.

The unit focuses on contact work, such as safe lifting techniques. Pupils are challenged to use a variety of contact ideas to suggest a dramatic storyline. At the heart of this unit is the ability to convey a sense of drama, depicting power, strength, courage and brutality. Pupils will learn to take responsibility for their own and others' safety when participating in work of this nature.

Choreographically, pupils concentrate on various forms of unison and canon, and group formations and pathways, in order to emphasise the dance idea. Pupils will create duet and small group work to depict aspects of the gladiators' personal traits, training regime and battles.

As they work, pupils will learn to appreciate the visual and expressive impact of different group formations and pathways in relation to the dance idea. They will also identify how elements of contact work reinforce the theme and how historic facts and events can be a stimulus for dance.

While this unit has an obvious appeal and physicality which many boys will enjoy, it has successfully been taught to girls and mixed groups. It is important to remember that girls must also be challenged to develop a strong sense of physicality. Although not well documented, female gladiator fights were commonplace and always a crowd pleaser.

## Resources

**Music**

- Main titles and Ape suite 2 of *Planet of the Apes*, (Varese Sarabande, 1997) film soundtrack.

**Video/DVD**

- *Gladiator* (Universal Pictures, 2004) and *Spartacus* (Criterion Collection, 2005) (these films have a certificate of 15 and PG. You should view the extracts first, to check their suitability).

**Additional Resources and Information**

For a quick and easy game, based on dressing gladiators for the arena (with excellent factual information), go to: www.bbc.co.uk/history/ancient/romans/launch_gms_gladiator.shtml

There are hundreds of websites relating to this theme. Below are listed some that contain both good images and factual information:

- http://en.wikipedia.org/wiki/Gladiator
- www.vroma.org
- www.murphsplace.com/gladiator/glads.html
- www.geocities.com/Athens/Stage/3591/gladiators.html
- www.salariya.com/web_books/gladiators/index/html
- http://depthome.brooklyn.cuny.edu/classics/gladiatr/index.htm

## Expectations

### Performance

- **Demonstrate gladiatorial characteristics and attitude** (eg imposing posture, serious facial expressions and a sense of pride).
- **Demonstrate clarity and precision in the use of dynamics** (eg sense of power, strength and tension).
- **Demonstrate clarity in the use of gestures to depict the different weapons** (eg clarity of shape and dynamic when slicing, cutting, swinging and stabbing).
- **Demonstrate technical skill and safe practice when working in contact with a partner** (eg control when taking partial and full weight during the mock-fight scenes).
- **Demonstrate accuracy when in close proximity to other dancers** (eg keeping accurate timing when in unison and canon and maintaining formations while travelling).

### Composition

- **Create movement for each section of the dance, using a range of contact ideas to communicate the narrative** (eg lifting a partner, using a partner as a base, assisting a partner's flight and over-powering a partner to show stylised gladiatorial battles).
- **Create 'fight' scenes for a highly stylised and tightly choreographed dance** (eg attention to phrasing, shape and adherence to guidelines).
- **Compose a dance using a mixture of sequential and accumulative canon and unison to add visual interest and dramatic impact** (eg select suitable points to stay in unison to accentuate the sense of power and unity, and use canon to reiterate and reinforce key images).

### Appreciation

- **Recognise how working in unison and how different forms of canon can contribute to the dramatic effect of a dance** (eg identify when and why unison/canon were used in their own and in others' dances).
- **Describe and analyse how knowledge of historic events can be used to add interest and authenticity to a dance** (eg how knowledge of the different weapons inspired different types of actions within the dance).
- **Identify factors of performance that contribute to convincing characterisation. Offer feedback to improve performance** (eg comment on and set targets related to confidence, concentration, conviction and focus).

## Coliseum

This unit culminates in a group dance that has a narrative structure (ie the story unfolds as the dance progresses). There are three sections to this dance – the main images and storyline of each section are outlined below:

### Section 1 – We are the gladiators

Main images and storyline:

- introducing the gladiators and their power, pride, honour and courage
- introducing the sense of group identity and common experiences shared by gladiators
- introducing the different types of weapons that gladiators use.

### Section 2 – Gladiator training

Main image and storyline: exploring different aspects of the gladiators' training (sparing joined by a pole and choreographed fight exercises).

### Section 3 – Inside the coliseum

Main images and storyline:

- entering the arena
- saluting the emperor
- fighting as a pack for survival
- fighting to the end!

## Section 1 – We are the gladiators

### Task 1

**Introducing the dance idea**

Watch the video extract from the film *Gladiator* that depicts gladiators as they enter the arena (approximately 1 hour 16 mins in or 1 hour 38 mins from the beginning of the opening credits. NB: if using a VHS video, you will need to reset the timer to nought at the beginning of the credits).

Note the following question on the board:

***Imagine you are about to fight in the coliseum in front of 50,000 people. How are you feeling?***

Facilitate the sharing of answers in response to the question and compile a list of key points on the board (eg frightened, excited, brave).

### Task 2

**Teacher-led short discussion on interesting facts about gladiators**

The purpose of this introductory discussion is to set the scene for the unit and to give pupils some background information on the life of a gladiator. These facts should help the pupils appreciate the historic context and harsh reality of the gladiators' existence. It is hoped that this information will generate interest, curiosity and a fascination that will engage pupils throughout the unit.

Teacher Prompt Sheet: Interesting Facts about Gladiators.

### Task 3

**Learning a set phrase for Section 1 – We are the gladiators**

a) Learning the set phrase

This phrase is a collage of images depicting:

- a sense of unity among gladiators
- the power, courage, pride and strength of the gladiator
- how different types of weapons were used.

To help with characterisation, you need to make constant reference to the motto, 'strength and honour', and to the gladiator's oath, 'Uri, vinciri, uerari, ferroque, necari' (to be burned, to be beaten, to die by the sword!).

Video Extract: Set Material – Gladiator Phrase.

The sample phrase is quite long; you are advised to either teach it over a number of weeks, select an appropriate section to use, or create your own phrase using material from the given example as a starting point.

b) Refining the set material within a block-group formation

Having learnt the set material, time should now be dedicated to practising and refining the technical and expressive skills inherent within the content. Pupils will need to be confident with the material before they can begin to develop aspects of timing and spacing.

Split the pupils into groups of six to perform, in unison and in a tight block formation, all facing the same direction. Discuss briefly with the pupils how working in unison can express the idea of the gladiators' power, strength and sense of group solidarity and purpose.

This material has been designed for groups of six but it works equally well in groups of four or eight, or for able groups of even larger numbers.

**Developing expressive skills**

In order to help develop pupils' expressive skills, they need to have a clear understanding of the choreographic intention (ie what they are trying to communicate, when they dance). As the teacher, you need to frequently remind the group of the link between the actions they are performing and what they are trying to communicate, and the mood, feeling and emotion within the dance. This guidance should allow pupils to 'get inside' the dance and to perform with integrity.

### Task 4

**Adapting the set material for a group by manipulating aspects of timing and spacing**

a) Using a demonstration group, illustrate how sequential and accumulative canon be used to enhance visual interest.

Sequential canon: one, two, three etc (as with a Mexican wave).

Accumulative canon: one, one plus two, one plus two plus three etc, or one and two, one and two plus three and four etc.

b) In their groups, get pupils to apply the principles of sequential and accumulative canon to the taught phrase.

As a result of these adaptations, opportunities to develop new and interesting pathways will arise (eg dancers might move through or around other dancers in the group). These adaptations should be encouraged; the intention is not that the taught material is adhered to rigidly: it is to be used as a baseline or springboard for pupils to build from.

c) Adopting the role of rehearsal director.

Once the group is near completion of the task, get pupils to take turns to be the rehearsal director; they should step out of the dance to watch and offer feedback to the group.

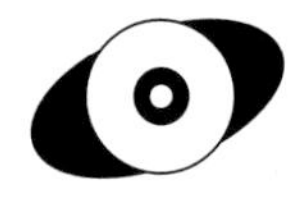

Teacher Prompt Sheet: What to Look for as Rehearsal Director.

**Introducing the role of the rehearsal director**

This strategy gives individual pupils the opportunity to step out of the group temporarily to adopt a leadership role. This challenges pupils to give appropriate feedback to improve the performance of their group and to communicate this feedback with confidence and clarity.

This strategy also gives teachers the opportunity to move around the class assessing pupils' evaluation skills (eg pupils' ability to observe accurately and describe movement using appropriate terminology).

Pupils should only be given a limited number of features on which to feedback. This will encourage them to be focused in their observation, rather than offering broad, general comments.

## Section 2 – Gladiator training

### Task 5

**Creating movement that depicts various aspects of the gladiators' training for use in Section 2**

This section is divided into three subsections, each focusing on a different aspect of the gladiators' training regime. Pupils must contribute their own ideas to each section within a framework of progressive tasks that you provide. Eventually, the sections will run seamlessly into one another with a transition from Section 1.

a) A brief discussion on gladiator training, supported by the gladiator film, *Spartacus*

Show the short scene in the training school, which is about 19 minutes from the beginning of the opening credits.

Teacher Prompt Sheet: Gladiator Training.

b) Training with the pole

Ask pupils to create a short phrase of movement with a partner, based on the idea of remaining a pole distance apart, as if training for close contact work. Explore ideas, such as creating a sense of tension between the fighters through the use of focus.

Partners should move around each other in a restricted space using basic travelling ideas. They must establish a sense of rhythm to the steps, for example:

- walking
- cross-over stepping
- turning while walking
- swaying from side to side while in a low second plié
- performing a step-close action.

Explain that partners must aim to stay in contact with one another; however, they can momentarily release and change grips to allow for turning and a greater range of movement, such as holding on to one another:

- at the shoulders with one or both hands
- by crossing held hands
- wrist to wrist
- elbow to elbow
- with a basket grip (each dancer holds their own wrist, eg right hand holds left wrist, left hand holds partner's right wrist).

As the phrase develops, encourage pupils to include changes of direction and to use the spare arm to reflect carrying a weapon.

c) Transition from Section 1 in to Section 2

Help pupils with the sequencing of material. To aid pupils' movement memory, it is a good idea to give each section of the dance a title. Before expecting pupils to add sections together, isolate the transition moment out for attention. Take some time to practise the last few movements from one section leading into the first few moments of the next section.

Suggested transition: at the end of Section 1, partners could move towards one another to stand side by side at on arm's length away from one another, with the inside arm resting on their partner's shoulder. They can then walk in contact into a new position to start Section 2.

d) Training exercises: Fight sequences

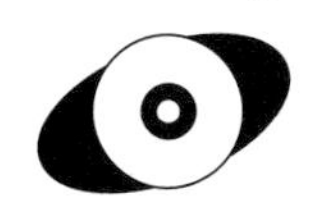

Pupil Worksheet: Gladiator Training – Starting Positions.

Pupils will eventually perform this part of Section 2 in duets in simultaneous unison, which will suggest the strict discipline and regimental approach of the gladiators' training. Each pair will, however, explore their own ideas first before sharing suggestions with the rest of the group.

**Step 1**

Select one photo on the worksheet for the group to copy. Pupils should concentrate on:

- the detail of the body positions
- the use of the free arm
- the focus between the dancers
- creating a sense of pressure, tension and resistance.

**Step 2**

Show the pupils other images to copy, concentrating on the details identified above.

**Step 3**

Each pair should select one image as the starting point for a phrase of movement and use the following structure to complete the phrase:

Move into the position (action); move in this position (reaction); move out of the position (resolution).

©Action Images/Reuters

Remind pupils about not being too literal and for the need for abstract movements to make it more dance-like, involving a range of body actions.

**Step 4**

Once happy that the pupils can perform this task sensibly and safely, ask each pair to extend their phrase to move into and out of other positions.

Encourage the following actions/images to be built into the phrase:

- stabbing
- blocking
- gripping
- lassoeing
- overpowering.

**Step 5**

Returning pupils to their groups of six, ask each pair to show their phrase to the group, then build a training fight sequence in which all three pairs perform the same material at the same time (in unison). The group must then select one of the following strategies:

- select one pair's phrase for the whole group to learn
- learn each other's phrase and perform them in sequence
- select the best bits from each pair's phrase and combine them into a new, extended phrase.

e) Five v One training

As an extension task, some groups could go on to explore a five versus one training scenario, where one dancer stands in the middle of a circle and fights off each opponent who comes at them in a random order. This scenario was used by gladiators to train their speed of response. To add to the challenge, no dancer can perform an action that a previous dancer has used.

Watch the video extract from the film *Gladiator* (about 20 minutes from the beginning of the opening credits).

**Preventing genuine bloodshed!**

It is obviously essential to keep a sense of order and discipline as the pupils work; attention to abstraction and tight structuring within tasks should ensure pupils stay focused. It is worth mentioning that all fight scenes in films are highly choreographed and that the director has a key role to play in designing the fight. Also, remind pupils that they are choreographing a dance; therefore, movement needs to be highly stylised. On this occasion, the use of a photographic work card, with a series of positions that pupils build phrases of movement around, as opposed to a 'free for all', serves to keep the pupils on task and thinking about stylising movement. The tight structuring of the task into action, reaction and resolution, and the discipline of three pairs performing the same duets at the same time (in unison) also helps keep pupils focused and retains a sense of order.

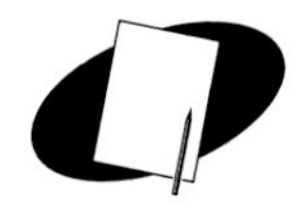

## Task 6

**Video analysis task: Group self-evaluation of technical and expressive skills as the basis for further improvement**

While the class works on Task 5d, get one group at a time to film their progress and to view their own work for a discussion of strengths and areas for development. Refer back to rehearsal director's notes used previously (Task 4c).

Following this, the groups need to be given further time to act on the areas for development identified.

## Task 7

**Short discussion tasks**

In order to deepen pupils' understanding of the dance idea, to create opportunities for cross-curricular learning and to develop aspects of citizenship, the following discussion topics can be used to generate interesting debate. Pupils will also be encouraged to consider their own moral response to similar modern-day situations.

Teacher Prompt Sheet: Gladiator Discussion Topics.

Topic 1 – The bloodiest displays of public amusement known to man.

Topic 2 – The case for and against female gladiators.

### Task 8

**Transition into Section 3 – In the Coliseum**

Ask pupils to create a short transition to go between the end of the training exercise fight sequence (Task 5d or 5e) and entering the arena. The storyline is that the gladiators enter the arena, promenade around the arena and then salute the emperor.

## Section 3: Inside the Coliseum

### Task 9

**Fighting as a pack**

**Step 1**

Instruct pupils to learn a short travelling phrase that they perform in their group of six, as a close pack. This reflects the moment in the film *Gladiator*, when Russell Crowe as Maximus suggests to his fellow gladiators that, to survive, they must stay close together. He states, *'whatever comes out of these gates, we've got a better chance of survival if we work together'* (approx 1 hour and 19 minutes from the beginning of the credits). In this section, the group are fighting an imaginary opposition.

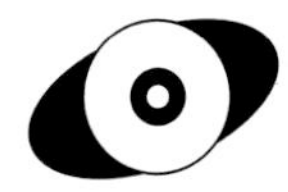

Video Extract: Set Material – Travelling as a Pack.

**Step 2**

Staying as a pack and in unison, ask pupils to extend the travelling phrase by adding some of the following:

- a surging forward as a pack to suggest attacking
- leaning slowly backwards as a group to suggest an overbearing force
- a sudden change of dynamics to suggest an unexpected attack
- circling as a group to suggest being surrounded
- a constant change of level and direction to suggest being attacked from all sides.

### Task 10

**Fighting to the end**

Now pupils have worked within tight structures and have learnt principles of safe contact work, they are ready to be set more open-ended choreographic tasks. For this final section, it is expected that pupils will draw upon the individual actions/phrases, which they have previously learned, for further development.

Suggested choreographic framework for fighting to the death: while pupils will have considerable freedom to interpret this section in their own way, it is advisable to provide a structure for them to explore within. The narrative is that they are now forced to fight the people they trained with if they are to stay alive.

Both trios travel towards one another and perform a short attacking phrase and then travel away from one another to re-group.

The group sub-divides into two. Both trios travel back towards one another and perform a different short attacking phrase. They then travel away from one another to re-group again.

As they come towards one another for the final time, the trio breaks up and a larger 'fight' occurs. This needs to include constantly changing group numbers (eg three v one, one v one, two v two).

Pupils must create an ending for their dance that has a clear storyline (eg only two gladiators remain alive; one gladiator is down and wounded and raises a hand, a sign of appealing for mercy, and the emperor decides their fate).

### Task 11

**Concluding questions**

Ask the question: if you were alive at the time, what role do you think you would have played? (eg would you have been a slave, a rich slave owner or even the emperor?)

# Unit 7: Grease Monkey (Year 9)

## About the Unit

This unit takes its inspiration from the opening scene of the professional dance work *The Car Man* (2001), choreographed by Matthew Bourne. The scene is set in a garage and depicts a group of car mechanics going about their daily work (car mechanics are sometimes known as 'grease monkeys'). The dance combines aspects of musical theatre with contemporary dance and uses Bizet's rousing classical score from the opera *Carmen*. Pupils will have the opportunity to use props, acting skills and dance movements together.

The unit focuses on developing the skill of music visualisation, using dramatic skills to portray a character and integrating the use of a prop effectively.

Choreographically, pupils concentrate on the use of motif development, and abstract working gestures alone and with others. They create material that integrates dance and drama and that demonstrates music visualisation.

As they work, pupils describe how they have used motif development to work from pedestrian, representational movement to symbolic, dance-like movement. Pupils identify key features the choreographer uses to help build and portray a character.

Using a professional work as a starting point is an exciting way for children to learn about and be inspired by dance. By watching the work of professional artists, pupils can learn about technique, expression and choreography. When using *The Car Man*, the intention is that pupils take the basic idea of the garage scenario and the nature and style of movement content to use as inspiration for their own interpretation of the idea. While it is desirable to try out some of the movement (as this will broaden pupil's vocabulary), it is important to go beyond mere replication of what they see. By the end of the unit, the work of each choreographic group should have its own individual identity.

### Resources

**Music**

Orchestral version, of Bizet's *Carmen*.

**Video/DVD**

*The Car Man* (Image Entertainment, 2001) by Matthew Bourne.

**Props**

A minimum of one car tyre per group and an assortment of other related props, such as brooms, newspapers, buckets, mugs and oily rags.

## Expectations

### Performance

- **Demonstrate appropriate characterisation when working alone and interacting with others** (eg through the appropriate use of gesture, posture and focus adopting the persona of a busy mechanic).
- **Demonstrate skilful use of props when dancing** (eg manipulate and integrate props, such as tyres and brooms, effectively and efficiently into their dance).
- **Demonstrate a sense of musicality when dancing** (eg show a direct correlation between the movement and the music with regard to the tempo, rhythm and dynamic phrasing).

### Composition

- **Structure material that integrates dance and drama skills seamlessly** (eg show smooth transitions into and out of the opening scene and when performing the short drama scenario).
- **Create material that demonstrates motif development as a tool to progress from representational to symbolic movement** (eg develop pedestrian, mechanical gestures, such as winding, pumping and pummelling, into dance-like phrases, by changing the size, rhythm and level of the actions being performed).
- **Create material that directly correlates to the music** (eg fit their mechanical gestures and travelling phrases into the tempo, rhythm and dynamic phrasing of the music).
- **Create movement that demonstrates various ways to manipulate a prop** (eg tyres that are rolled, thrown and passed around the body, and brooms that are swept rhythmically and passed between dancers).

### Appreciation

- **Pupils know the difference between representational and symbolic movement** (eg they are able to describe how they have used motif development to work from pedestrian, representational movement to symbolic dance).
- **Pupils identify key features that the choreographer uses to help build and portray a character** (eg how the use of posture, focus and gesture can be used to portray a mechanic).
- **Pupils identify elements of production that contribute to the expression of the dance idea** (eg being able to describe how the set, costume and use of props suggest the time, place and storyline).

## Grease Monkey

This unit culminates in a group dance that combines aspects of musical theatre and contemporary dance. It follows a loose narrative structure in which pupils have opportunities to develop their own storylines within a given framework.

### Task 1

**Introducing the dance idea**

a) Share information about *The Car Man* and the work of the choreographer Matthew Bourne with the group.

Teacher prompt sheet: Key facts about *The Car Man* (2001) and Matthew Bourne, the choreographer.

b) Explain that the unit focuses on the first section of the dance only. It is set in a garage and portrays a group of mechanics at work. Before observing the first section of the video, ask the class the following questions:

- What are the typical actions you would see a mechanic doing (eg pummelling, polishing, wrenching)?
- If you were going to audition dancers for the role of a mechanic, what qualities would you look for (eg a dancer that shows physical strength and someone who would not mind getting their hands dirty)?

### Task 2

**Video observation**

a) Show pupils the opening scene of *The Car Man*, up to the point when the bells sound to indicate the end of the working day. As they watch, ensure pupils look for the actions and characteristics they identified in Task 1b.

b) Facilitate discussion, summarising key points on the board.

c) Introduce the concepts of representational and symbolic movement (ie representational movement is in real time and like acting. Symbolic movement is where the essence of the action has been abstracted to make it more dance-like).

d) Show pupils the video for the second time and ask them to look for examples of representational and symbolic working actions (eg representational actions would include polishing the car and wiping their hands on oily rags; symbolic actions would include winding, steering and pummelling, which they show in an exaggerated way and while they are performing dance-like leaps, jumps and turns).

**Guiding pupils to watch professional works on film**

The use of film, as a resource for learning and teaching in dance, is well established. To make video observation a positive and worthwhile experience, you need to consider the following:

- Keep extracts short.
- Permit pupils to view the extract several times.
- Keep commentary to a minimum, only pointing out key features.
- Provide pupils with a minimum number of specific points to focus on at one time.
- Progress from questions that only require description (eg what happens? how many?) to those that ask for analysis and interpretation (eg what, why and how?)

### Task 3

**Choreographing the opening image**

Split pupils into groups of six and make them aware of the importance of a strong and clear opening image. It should instantly set the scene for the audience by helping to establish who the characters are and where the action is taking place.

Instruct pupils to create an opening image, thinking about:

- how the group can be sub-divided down and spread around the dance space (eg three plus two plus one)
- how the dancers might adopt different roles to give the scene a sense of realism (eg two dancers might read the paper, while others work)
- how the props might be used
- how the use of different levels can add visual interest.

For the opening section, the content should be kept representational and call upon the pupils' acting skills.

## Task 4

**Creating a duet phrase: working actions of the mechanic**

By the end of the task, each choreographic group will have created a bank of material that the group can adapt, develop and structure.

a) Divide the groups of six into smaller groups (eg three groups of two, two groups of three, or a group of four and a group of two).

b) Each sub-group selects three working actions to perform repeatedly and then, on your command, changes from one to the next.

c) Pupils decide the number of repetitions of each movement. You should then direct pupils to refine the detail of the movement (eg to show the effort required to pump and the impulse shown in a polishing action).

d) Explain how pupils will use a process called motif development as a tool to make representational movement abstract.

e) Pupils explore the development of spatial features. Taking their three working actions, pupils experiment with changing the size of the actions (eg enlarging movements and experimenting with a mixture of small, medium and large).

f) Pupils explore the development of action features. Taking their three working actions, pupils experiment with adding further actions while performing the working action (eg adding a roll, a jump, or a leap).

g) Pupils explore the development of dynamic features. Taking their three working actions, pupils experiment with the rhythm and speed of the actions (eg so that the working actions fit into the phrasing of the music).

h) Give each sub-group time to select and structure a short phrase that illustrates at least three working actions that have been developed from representational to symbolic movement.

i) Each sub-group shares its phrases with the rest of the group. The group should then decide how to link the phrases to the opening image. The simplest way would be for the sub-groups to perform their phrases simultaneously. More able pupils may wish to teach each other their phrases to extend their material.

j) In whole groups, get the pupils to practise linking the opening image with their working action phrases.

## Task 5

**Learning set material**

In order to further extend pupils' movement vocabulary and offer a contrast to the more drama-based content, pupils need to learn the set material, which includes various travelling movements that can be integrated into their dance. The material includes jumping, sliding, leaping, galloping, rolling, stepping and running, stylised to show the Spanish matador influence, mixed with the gestures of a mechanic.

Video Extract: Set Material – Grease Monkey.

## Task 6

**Video observation: The use of background and foreground**

a) Show pupils the opening section of *The Car Man* again, focusing on the concept of background and foreground (eg how background action is less significant to what is happening in the foreground. The foreground provides the main focus for the audience and is where all the main action happens; the background sets the scene and helps with the narrative).

b) Once pupils have learned the set material, the group should decide how to use this material within their dance. Pupils decide which parts of the set material to include, in what order, where to perform them on the stage and how many dancers will perform them at any one time. This section of the dance should show the design concept of background and foreground (eg while some group members perform the travelling phrases in the foreground, others continue to perform more representational/drama-like actions in the background). Pupils should take account of audience perspective and, in doing so, appoint a rehearsal director to consider points, such as:

- Are the dancers in the background too dominant and is their movement distracting?
- Can you see all the dancers?
- Does their spatial arrangement communicate the feel of a working garage?

### Task 7

**Analysing the production elements**

Together, you and the pupils complete the production elements analysis chart. This chart is designed to develop pupils' awareness of the contribution that set, props and costume make to the expression of the dance idea.

Pupil Worksheet: Grease Monkey – Production Elements Analysis Chart.

### Task 8

**Creating an acting episode**

Musical theatre is often a mixture of acting and dancing. Pupils devise a short drama episode that is woven into their dance. The acting episode should communicate an incident that occurs in the garage, for example:

- the boss arrives back from a meeting early to find the mechanics lazing around
- a tyre is clumsily dropped onto someone's foot, leading to an argument
- the pupils come up with an idea of their own.

Pupils will need to consider the use of gesture and focus as an essential part of communication and make their acting episode convincing. Groups will also need to decide what leads up to this incident and how it is resolved.

### Task 9

**Creating a transition**

From the resolution of the episode, pupils create a short transition that depicts the mechanics returning to work on the car, either all at the same time or one after the other.

### Task 10

**Group phrase: working actions around a single car using the props**

Returning to the type of material created in Task 4, pupils create a new section depicting all the mechanics working around a single car. Pupils may repeat or rework material from the earlier section or create new material.

You could ask pupils to consider ideas where one person is under the car and four other dancers are working on the wheels, while the remaining dancer directs the proceedings. Alternatively, one of the props may become the central feature of the work, with a tyre being passed in different ways between the mechanics.

### Task 11

**Creating a finale**

At the start of the final section, pupils return to the set travelling phrases, this time having decided which steps and in which order the material should be performed, with the number of dancers gradually increasing (accumulative canon). The groups must plan at what point each dancer will join in. Ultimately, all dancers will be performing in unison to create a climax to the dance. Pupils should decide the final ending image; this might have a sudden dramatic stop to symbolise the end of the working day or a gradual return to work.

### Task 12

**Making rehearsal notes and refining the dance ready for performance**

Ask each group to compile a set of rehearsal notes. Groups to select two rehearsal directors who, in turn, watch the group and provide feedback on the targets set. (This task works best when combined with video analysis.)

To create a sense of occasion, pupils may wish to add to the overall impact of their performance with the use of costume.

### Task 13

**Pupils share their final performance with the class**

# Unit 8: My Name is Cocaine (Year 9)

## About the Unit

This unit uses the poem entitled *My Name is Cocaine* as its stimulus. Pupils will learn how to create and develop material that communicates a powerful message, such as the dangers of drug addiction.

We are suggesting this unit is taught towards the end of Year 9. Firstly, it demands that the pupils draw upon the knowledge and skills taught previously and, secondly, it tackles a serious contemporary social issue. The stimulus is a thought-provoking poem; therefore, the maturity of the pupils and their ability to respond in a sensitive manner is important. This unit works best alongside a well-researched and factual drug-education programme. It will dispel myths about drug addiction, and generate lively and controversial discussion.

The unit focuses on revisiting the use of contact work, at a more advanced level. Pupils explore lifting, throwing and catching and look at sustained close contact work. Attention to the characteristics of the drug and its effect on the behaviour and emotional state of the addict provide both the narrative for the dance and the focus for the development of expressive skills.

Choreographically, pupils explore developing a narrative, while working in a relatively abstract way. Physical challenges that explore ways to manipulate a partner form the basis of improvisations. Material is then set, adapted and extended for a small group. The structure of the dance follows the development and climax of the poem.

As they work, pupils should discuss the poem and how it can be interpreted and expressed through movement. Pupils will explain their choice of movements in relation to the dance idea, and should be able to analyse and evaluate their own and others' work.

**Note**

The key priority for this unit is for pupils to use dance as a medium to express their thoughts and feelings about a serious social issue. Alongside the challenges of creating the dance, are opportunities to discuss concerns relating to drugs. You need to be prepared for honest, open discussion and be armed with correct factual information.

You need to help pupils avoid falling into the trap of making material that is melodramatic or relies on obvious pedestrian gestures (eg mime-like actions of injecting and snorting!). Pupils need to be guided to take these key images and abstract them.

### Resources

**Music**

- 'Prime Audio Soup' from *The Matrix* (Maverick, 1999) soundtrack.
- 'Under the influence' on *Surrender* (Astrelwerks, 1999) by The Chemical Brothers.
- 'The Heat' on *Birdy* (Geften Records, 2002) soundtrack.

**Video**

- *Swansong* (English National Ballet, 2004).

**Additional Resources and Information**

For useful information and resources aimed at teenagers specifically, go to 'Tips for Teens' at www.health.org/govpubs/phd640i/Tips for teens

## Expectations

### Performance

- **Demonstrate correct technique in advanced contact work** (eg lifting, pitching and catching with ease, showing an awareness of the need for core stability).
- **Demonstrate clarity and precision in the use of extreme and subtle dynamics** (eg power in explosive jumps and kicks, in contrast to the use of impulsive, fluid and successive movements).
- **Demonstrate an appropriate use of focus and facial expression to enhance communication of the dance idea** (eg use focus and facial expression to show the contrasting relationships between the drug and the addict, such as tempting and teasing/overpowering and intimidating).

### Composition

- **Create movement that demonstrates various ways to manipulate a partner while maintaining the role of addict or drug** (eg various ways to block, overpower, lift and latch on to a partner).
- **Develop movement in groups, through adapting and reworking initial duets** (eg repeat, re-order and embellish the original duets).
- **Create movement that is rich in dynamic contrast and builds to a climax to enhance communication of the dance idea** (eg use of pushing, pulling and snatching compared with caressing and cradling, which builds in speed, tension and intensity).

### Appreciation

- **Identify, describe and interpret key images from the poem that have the potential for movement** (eg 'if you try me one time, you will never be free' suggests you could be restrained and are attempting to break free).
- **Discuss the social issues surrounding the poem and how this is demonstrated in the dance** (eg describe the changing emotions felt by the addict and as the poem progresses and how these are mirrored in the dance).
- **Evaluate the success of other groups in communicating the dance idea** (eg summarise how the groups depict the various relationships between the drug and the addict).

## My Name is Cocaine

This unit culminates in a group dance, of which there are four sections: Section 1 includes the initial duet work; Section 2, the set material performed individually; and in Section 3, dancers return to their duets, and the material is shared, reworked and developed to create a new duet that the whole group perform in unison. The dance concludes with the group depicting a range of outcomes for the drug addict.

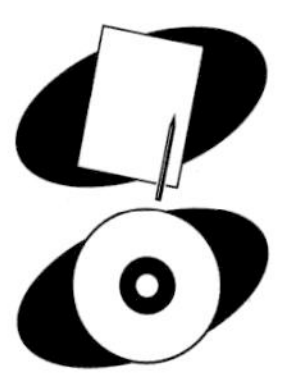

### Task 1

**Introducing the dance idea**

Pupil Worksheet: My Name is Cocaine.

Read the poem with the pupils and discuss the following:

- What is your initial reaction to the poem?
- What aspects of it stick out clearly in your mind?
- What do you think are the clear messages?
- What do you visualise when you read it?

### Task 2

**Providing pupils with key factual information about cocaine addiction and facilitating discussion on the common characteristics of cocaine and drug addiction**

Teacher Prompt Sheet: Cocaine Addiction – The Facts.

### Task 3

**Creating a bank of words with potential for movement**

In pairs, ask the pupils to revisit the poem and think about the key relationship features between the addict and the drug (eg how do they interact? Who has control?).

Each pair must make a list of words, such as:

| aggressive | in pain | persuasive | trapped |
|---|---|---|---|
| angry | irritated | persistent | unaware |
| ashamed | lonely | pouncing | wrapping |
| clinging-on | manipulative | pulling | around |
| creeping | nervous | pushing | |
| curious | on-the-edge | relieved | |
| enticing | out-of-control | sad | |
| fearful | over- | sense-of-calm | |
| frustrated | powering | teasing | |
| hovering | | tired | |

### Task 4

**Creating a duet**

Having identified a list of key words, the pupils are now ready to create short phrases of movement to be used within a duet, depicting various relationships between the addict and the drug. One dancer is to represent the drug, the other the addict.

a) Show pupils examples of phrases that illustrate trapping, grabbing and restraining the addict. It is not the intention that pupils learn this material, but use it as a springboard for creating their own ideas.

Video Extract: Example Material – Stopping and Grabbing the Addict.

b) Suggested starting points for the phrases are as follows:

**Phrase 1**

Dancers stand one behind the other; the one playing the addict in the front and the other, playing the drug, behind. The 'drug dancer' traps the addict from behind (eg they might trap with one or both arms around the waist or knees, lock under the shoulder, pull the addict's hands behind their back or cut in front of their space, preventing them from moving forwards). The phrase should grow in intensity and speed and gradually move off the spot.

As pupils work, reinforce the need for changing dynamics to show the various ways that the drug can take hold. Each duet should show the difference between the smooth and enticing nature of the drug in contrast with its possessive and persistent side.

**Phrase 2**

The next challenge is to create a travelling phrase that suggests the addict breaking away. The drug is too powerful and repeatedly stops the addict. (Use examples from the DVD to assist with this, or encourage pupils to think of other ways of stopping their partners.)

This travelling action will then need to be built into the duet. Allow the pair to decide where in the dance it will go; however, pupils must justify its place within the phrase (eg the stopping or grabbing may come right at the very beginning of the duet, in order to create maximum impact from the start and to allow the audience to establish the relationship. In contrast to this, it could be woven into the middle section of the duet, to depict the addict wanting to get away but that the power of the drug is too strong).

As the pairs work on creating their dance, ask them to consider the following:

- **focus and projection** – to reinforce the idea of power
- **changing levels** – to reinforce the idea of drug-enforced highs and lows
- **altering the pathways** – to reinforce the idea of anxiety
- **small gestural actions** – to communicate taking the drug
- **repetition** – to show the concept of being hooked on the drug
- **spatial variation** – to show the constant battle between the person and their addiction.

## Task 5

**Observing an extract from a professional work**

a) Pupils watch the opening section of *Swansong* by Christopher Bruce, which depicts a scene of a prisoner being intimidated by two guards. (While the context for the dance is different, similar skills are used by the choreographer to help the audience appreciate the relationship between the dancers.)

Guide pupils to notice how the use of focus, proximity, concentration and facial expression enhance communication of the dance idea. These factors help set the scene, establishing clearly for the audience the relationship between the performers.

b) Pupils should consider how they can use what they have seen in *Swansong* to improve their own dance.

c) Give the pupils time to improve and develop their duets.

## Task 6

**Observation task**

Pupil Worksheet: My Name is Cocaine – Choreographic Evaluation of Duet.

Pupils should observe another pair performing their dance. Observers must focus on a combination of performance and choreographic features of the dance and use the worksheet to note their feedback. Pupils should be encouraged to give positive and constructive feedback with clear targets for improvement. Give time for the corrections to be worked on before they are reviewed again by the same observers for signs of improvement.

## Task 7

**Developing the material into a group dance (four or six dancers)**

Building on from the initial duets, this section of the dance focuses specifically on the point at which the drug takes hold of an addict. Dancers should perform this section in unison, starting on a diagonal line. The diagonal line represents a line of cocaine. Unison is used to suggest the strength and power the drug has and how, when it 'kicks-in', there is a common experience, regardless of social class, age and gender.

a) Transition from duet into diagonal line:

Each duet should finish with the addict being pulled, pushed or dragged across the space and with the group in the diagonal line.

b) Taught phrase:

Give the pupils time to learn the taught phrase from the video or from yourself.

Key motifs within the taught phrase include:

- constantly changing from being in the air to on the floor, to suggest drug-induced highs and lows
- moving around on the floor and passing through an arched position, to suggest the cravings
- the 'wiping gesture', to suggest the pathway of the drug around the body.

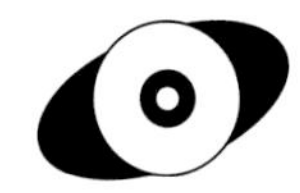

Video extract: Set Material – My Name is Cocaine.

## Task 8

**Creating additional material, beginning with duets in unison for the whole group to perform**

This section explores how individual victims deal with their addiction and the final consequences for each addict. The section begins with simultaneous duets and then progresses to movement that is unique to each pair.

a) Returning to their initial duet, ask pairs to show their work to the rest of the group.

b) Groups must then create a new, shared duet that is a hybrid of the best bits of their previous duets.

As the material is reformed, pupils should be encouraged to develop the group vocabulary further by adding their own ideas.

c) To finish the dance, each pair within the group should make their own ending that clearly shows the outcome for the addict. Each pair will need to consider:

- what they are trying to communicate (eg the addict slowly becoming less dependent)
- which movements best show this (eg repeated pulling actions that get the addict further away from the drug each time)
- how the use of dynamics and focus help communicate their intention (eg the dance may finish with a final glance back at other addicts still hooked on the drug).

**Dealing with able pupils**

The challenge for the teacher is to meet the needs of all pupils. A common and successful strategy is to get the more able dancers in the class to share their knowledge and skills with the less able. However, it is also important for the teacher to challenge the most able, who should sometimes be permitted to work together and be encouraged to create work that stretches and challenges them. The entire class will benefit from seeing exemplary work as this will provide them with a visual model to aspire to.

## Task 9

While creating this new duet, pupils could consider the following:

- transporting their partner across the space
- moving across the space without breaking contact, showing resistance
- Including catches which show an exaggerated flight phase.

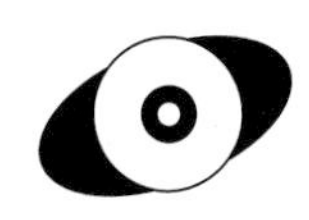

Video Extracts: Set Material – Extension Tasks.

**Preparation for examination work**

As this is one of the final units within the scheme, it is advisable to take the time to give pupils an opportunity to sample aspects of examinations in dance. By making direct links with the specification, you can help the pupils gain an insight into the type of knowledge, understanding and expectations required at examination level.

This unit highlights many of the main choreographic elements that pupils will go on to study (eg how to analyse a stimulus for movement potential, how choreographic devices are selected in relation to the dance idea and how movement material can be revisited, reworked and developed). Constant and explicit reference should be made to these throughout the unit.

©Alan Edwards

# Unit 9: Cyber (Year 9)

## About the Unit

This unit challenges pupils to perform and create movement that uses the body in unconventional ways. It takes as its stimulus the concepts of **cyberspace** (the environment in which communication occurs over computer networks) **cybernetics** (the science of automatic control systems) and **cyborg** (a fictional person who can move beyond human limitations by mechanical elements built into the body). These factors impact on the way pupils will move and how they will structure and create material.

The unit focuses on challenging pupils' coordination. Pupils must master complex and unusual combinations of body actions. These actions give the illusion of being inhuman by using a combination of disjointed movement and unusual pathways of energy through the body.

Choreographically, pupils experiment with unconventional strategies, such as various chance procedures based on the arbitrary selection of numbers, computer commands and designing their own dance score.

As they work, pupils should analyse and describe the movements of their peers and of professional dancers. They must explain the impact of the choreographic strategies used on the resulting movement vocabulary. In addition, they will translate computer language into dance-specific instructions for their own choreographic tasks.

**Dare to be different?**

The core of this unit encourages pupils to develop a spirit for experimentation. Pupils are challenged to put aside conventional ways of moving, creating and structuring dance. It is important that the teacher is seen to encourage attempts to be different. Some pupils may initially find the movements hard to perform and remember, or think that the actions are ugly and not dance-like. Likewise, they may feel the choreography lacks logic as it does not have a narrative structure. Constantly reminding pupils of the need for choreographers to 'invent' new ways of moving, which reflect the 'cyber era', along with the satisfaction gained through mastery of the physical challenges, should alleviate this.

### Resources

**Music**

- Dael, c/pach on *Tri Repetae* (Tut, 1996) by Autechre.
- 'Dub Gusset' on *Rhythm and Stealth* (Sony, 1999) by Leftfield.
- 'Technologic' on *Human After All* (Virgin Records, 2005) by Daft Punk.

**Additional Resources and Information**

For further information about Wayne McGregor and the Random Dance Company, visit www.randomdance.org

For related information on Cyborgs, go to http://en.wikipedia.org/wiki/Cyborg

## Expectations

### Performance

- **Demonstrate coordination in complex combinations of body actions** (eg hip jutting out at the same time as the shoulder circles, ribcage shifting in one direction at the same time as the knee buckles, or a sequential series of disjointed movements).
- **Demonstrate accurate movement memory when performing unusual patterns of movement** (eg performing the telephone phrase smoothly and consistently).
- **Demonstrate clear pathways of energy through the body** (eg a smooth successive flow of energy, in contrast to a jolting, nudging ricochet of energy).

### Composition

- **Demonstrate a willingness and courage to try alternative ways to create material** (eg perseverance when creating the telephone phrase and a positive attitude when using the dance score).
- **Create original movement responses using chance procedures** (eg responses to the actions on the movement menu are unique and imaginative).
- **Create novel interpretations of the key computer commands alone and with a partner** (eg make inventive ways to scan, attach, eject and rotate).

### Appreciation

- **Identify and describe key stylistic features of the professional work observed** (eg disjointed action, inhuman appearance and erratic phrasing).
- **Articulate the choreographic process experienced and compare and contrast this with previous choreographic experiences** (eg describe similarities and differences between their cyber dance and one other).
- **Evaluate the success of other groups in communicating the dance idea** (eg evaluate the originality of the movement, the appropriate dynamic content for the computer commands and the overall effectiveness of the final dance).

## Cyber

This unit culminates in a duet or quartet. The duet or quartet contains two blocks of material, created from different choreographic processes, and two travelling phrases. Pupils use this material to create their own dance score, in which they decide the order and structure of the final dance.

### Task 1

**Introducing the dance idea**

Provide a brief introduction, explaining that this unit will challenge the pupils to perform and create movements that use the body in unconventional ways and takes as its starting point various cyber-related concepts.

### Task 2

**Video observation: cyber solo with accompanying question**

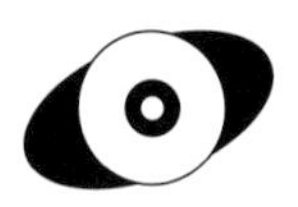

Video Extract: Example Material – Cyber Solo.

The cyber solo illustrates how the body can be used in unusual ways and depicts a human body with mechanical elements built into it. Ask pupils to answer the following question:

What is it about the way the dancer moves that makes him look part human, part mechanical? (For example, the unusual shapes the body makes, the erratic succession of actions and the unusual coordination of body parts.)

### Task 3

**Completing the movement directory**

Pupil Worksheets: Movement Directory and Movement Menu Worksheets.

Ask pupils to match up their telephone number with the corresponding actions from the movement menu.

### Task 4

**Creating Block 1: Building an original phrase of movement (telephone phrase)**

This process, and the resulting movement content, has the potential to be quite complex. Below are a number of differentiated options for the practical work:

- In pairs, ask pupils to make a phrase of movement based on one dancer's telephone number.
- Individually, get pupils to make a phrase of movement based on their own telephone number.
- Individually, ask pupils to make a phrase of movement based on their own telephone number. Then, get the pupils to join up with a partner, learn each other's phrase and perform them one after the other.
- In pairs, ask pupils to retain the first three digits (three actions) and to perform these alongside each other in union. Then, ask the pupils to join the last three digits of their telephone numbers together (six actions) and to re-order these actions to create a new phrase. Link the first three actions and the re-ordered actions together (nine actions in total).

The Movement Directory worksheet gives pupils instructions, such as the importance of moving from one action directly into the next and what to do when they see a pause or fast-forward symbol.

The task has been designed to facilitate original movement vocabulary.

Restricting pupils from always coming back to a neutral standing position (in between the actions) encourages pupils to find new connections between movements and, as a result, more original responses.

As the pupils work, select and share good examples of unusual responses to the actions on the menu.

### Task 5

**Refining the created phrase(s)**

Having created their material, time should now be dedicated to practising and refining the technical and expressive skills inherent within the content.

Give the pupils structured practice time to focus on:

- **clarity of dynamic contrasts** – particular attention should be given to the tension and weight of different actions (eg flicking, rebounding, and showing tension and release in robotic/popping movements)
- **clarity of action when moving at speed** – particular attention should be given to completing each action and making a direct connection to the next action.

### Task 6

**Block 2 – Building a second movement phrase (computer commands phrase)**

a) Give the pupils time to listen to the lyrics of 'Technologic' by Daft Punk and complete the Computer Commands/Movement worksheet.

Pupil Worksheet: Computer/Movement Commands.

Teacher Answer Sheet: Computer/Movement Commands.

b) Explain how the taught material is based on actions that represent physical interpretations of selected computer commands on the worksheet (eg scan, eject, insert and rotate) and, in addition, movements that emphasise action at the joints (eg flexing and rotating knees, elbows, hips and shoulders).

c) Give the pupils time to learn the taught material: computer commands.

Video Extract: Set Material – Computer Commands.

d) Ask pupils to identify movements within the taught material that represent the command 'eject' and explain the features of the movement (eg the jump at the beginning of the phrase, which goes from two feet to one foot with a strong nudging action with the elbow. The jump has a sudden explosive quality that suggests a disc being ejected from a computer).

e) Encourage pupils to explore different ways to represent the command 'eject'.

As pupils work, prompt them to think about the various ways they could do this (eg taking weight onto their hands and pushing their hips suddenly into the air; a single body part performing a short sudden movement or a slide across the floor).

f) Lead a short, guided improvisation task based on the command, 'rotate'.

The image behind the task is based on how a photo can be rotated/inverted in various directions on a computer.

- Pupils should select an angular starting position, which emphasises the joints.
- On your command, pupils must select a different angular position, perhaps at a different level or emphasising different body parts (this process is repeated a few times to encourage pupils to move beyond their first, most obvious response).
- Ask pupils to select their 'best' angular position and attempt to rotate the shape to face new directions. Provide prompts, such as: can you flip the photo upside down? Can you rotate the photo 180 degrees or 360 degrees?
- Pupils should now explore transitions between the various images, resulting in a short phrase that shows the main images from different angles.

g) In pairs, get pupils to share their best ideas for ejecting and rotating and, together, create a short phrase that includes a mixture of both. Pupils should perform this in unison.

h) Ensure pupils add the short rotating and ejecting phrase to the beginning of the taught material.

## Task 7

**Refining the extended set material**

Having learnt/created their material, time should now be dedicated to practising and refining the technical and expressive skills inherent within the content.

Give pupils structured practice time to focus on the:

- **clarity of dynamic contrasts** – particular attention should be given to the tension and weight of different actions (the slow, firm and sustained scanning action, the punching, stabbing inserting action and unexpected and staccato ejecting actions)
- **precision in the shape of the image that is rotated**
- **accuracy of timing between the two dancers.**

## Task 8

**Developing the relationship aspects of the extended taught material**

a) Discuss commands from the worksheet that suggest ways in which dancers can physically relate to one another (eg 'scan, attach and drag').

b) Using video examples, demonstrate how the idea of scanning and attaching can be translated into movement.

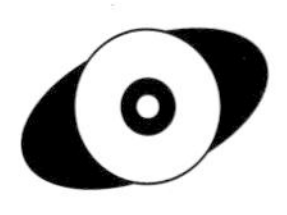

Video Extract: Example Material – Scanning and Attaching.

c) Give the pupils time to explore ways to 'scan' their partner. Dancer A could hold a position from the phrase while Dancer B traces the shape. As pupils work, provide prompt statements to encourage their experimentation, such as:

- try starting your scanning from different points (eg the scanning could start from behind, in front or at the side)
- try starting the scanning from left to right and back or from the middle
- try using different body parts to scan (eg elbows, knee or head).

d) Ask the pupils to swap roles.

© Random Dance (photo by Ravi Deepres)

e) Encourage pupils to explore ways to find points of **attachment** to their partner. For example, hooking on, wrapping around, leaning on, and laying over or on.

- Dancer A selects a position from the taught material.
- Dancer B attaches him or herself. While in contact, both dancers attempt to perform the next movement of the phrase (it may be necessary to adapt the movement).
- Dancer A **sends** the attachment away.

As pupils work, provide prompt statements to encourage experimentation and ensure safe contact work, for example:

- Try starting your attachment from different points (eg the attachment could start from behind, in front or at the side).
- Try attaching the same body part (eg forearm to forearm, or different body parts).
- Try sending the attachment away at speed.

f) Ask pupils to swap roles.

g) Get pupils to build short phrases that incorporate various ways to **scan** and **attach**. The roles should constantly swap throughout. (As an extension task, some pupils might like to go on to explore the concept of **drag**.)

h) Add the short phrase to the end of the taught material.

### Task 9

**Learning travelling phrases**

The material created so far, despite being very complex in nature, may well be relatively stationary. The travelling phrases will provide movement and spatial contrast.

The image behind the travelling phrases is the interweaving network of wires, cables and satellite waves. The phrases show sudden surges of energy that reroutes frequently to change direction. Select the travelling phrases on the video that you wish to teach.

Video Extracts: Set Material – Travelling Phrases.

### Task 10

**Structuring a cyber dance**

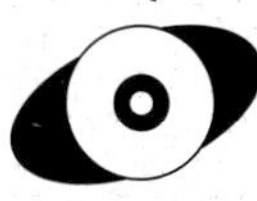

Pupil Worksheet: Structuring your Cyber Dance.

Instruct pupils to use the worksheet as a dance score. This will help them with decisions about how to structure their material into their final dance.

### Task 11

**Whole class sharing and filming final performances**

### Task 12

**Discussing the dance**

Each group must plan a five-minute presentation that focuses on their choreographic processes and the key aspects of their dance. The group may use clips from their videoed performance or show individual actions/phrases to demonstrate how material has been developed. When presenting to the class, pupils should cover some of the following points:

- how the dance has been structured
- how their movements relate to the dance idea (eg by clearly depicting computer commands)
- how their movements use the body in unusual ways
- the key choreographic devices used
- how the space has been used
- aspects that are particularly strong
- aspects that need further development
- aspects they found particularly challenging and how they resolved them.

**Getting pupils talking about dance**

In addition to dancing and choreographing, it is important that pupils can talk articulately about dance, using appropriate vocabulary. Talking about dance should go beyond merely stating likes and dislikes; pupils should be able to describe in detail and discuss, analyse, compare, contrast, interpret and evaluate their own and others' work. Questions should be asked and tasks devised that require pupils to give more than a simple yes/no response. You need to give pupils sufficient thinking time to prepare their answers, persevere when pupils give limited responses and find many ways to phrase the same question to assist pupils' understanding.

# Warming Up in Dance

A warm-up in dance should include:

- **activities to quicken the heart rate, increase blood flow to muscles and raise the body's core temperature** (eg general locomotion actions, such as running, skipping and step patterns, and/or actions like swinging and lunging, which use major muscle groups)
- **movements that mobilise the spine** (eg exercises or phrases of movement that include stretching, curling, twisting, arching and tilting)
- **movements that increase the range of motion around the joints and the flexibility of the muscles** (eg exercises or phrases of movement that include arm/leg circling and swinging actions, pliés and deep lunges)
- **opportunities to rehearse/refine motor patterns and aspects of technical or expressive skills required later in the lesson** (eg a dance lesson that focuses on elevation would typically begin with pliés and rises to reinforce correct technique)
- **opportunities to introduce new material and revise or consolidate existing material**, related to or drawn from the units of work
- **movements that reflect the prominent style/focus of the unit** (eg in dance it would be inappropriate to begin with a street-dance style warm-up, when the prominent style of the lesson/unit is contemporary)
- **reference to technical and expressive skills** (eg attention to correct posture, alignment and use of focus).

**Notes**

- Aspects of the above can be combined into repeatable phrases of movement, with/without musical accompaniment.
- Phrases that move through dynamic stretching are preferable to static stretching, focusing on isolated muscles.
- Opportunities to introduce simple compositional principles (eg pupils choosing the order in which to perform four given actions) can be built into warm-ups.

# Movement Analysis: Action, Space, Dynamic and Relationships

| Action (What?) | Dynamic (How?) – Qualities of Movement |
|---|---|
| • Bend/stretch, twist.<br>• Transference of weight from body part to body part.<br>• Travel (eg walk, run, roll, slide, skip).<br>• Turn.<br>• Gesture – a movement without weight (eg nod, wave, point).<br>• Five basic jumps (eg one to one foot [hop], one to other [leap], two to two feet [jump], one to two feet [assemble] and two feet to one foot [sissonne]).<br>• Balance.<br>• Body parts (eg use of feet, elbows, knees, torso, fingers). | • Time – speed (eg suddenly, rapidly, accelerating, slowly, gradually, leisurely).<br>• Weight – degrees of tension, amount of strength, use of gravity (eg relaxed, firm, rigid, delicate, suspended, swinging, falling).<br>• Space – how energy is released through space. Pathway of energy (eg directly, flexibly).<br>• Flow – amount of control/freedom in the release of energy so movement can be stopped at any time (eg abandoned, ongoing, stoppable, staccato, smooth).<br>Attention to rhythm arises from the study of dynamics.<br>When analysing dynamics, it is the combination of the above that gives the full range of possibilities (eg a strong, sudden and direct movement compared to a light, flexible and indirect movement). For example:<br>Hesitant, flowing, explosive, calmly, pulsating, restrained, percussive, melting, cutting, slicing, punching, boisterous, poised, swishing, pressing. |
| **Spatial (Where?)** | **Relationship (With Whom or What?)** |
| • Size (eg small, expanding, shrinking).<br>• Shape (eg angular, curved, straight, thin, wide, round, twisted, asymmetrical).<br>• Level (eg low, medium, high).<br>• Pathway - floor and air (eg zigzag, circular, straight, spiral).<br>• Direction (eg forwards, sideways, diagonal).<br>• Proximity (eg near, far).<br>• Group shape/formations (eg circle, diamond, random, triangle, clump). | • Alone, with others or with object or set.<br>• Group work (eg numerical variations, spatial variations, group shape).<br>• Spatial relationships (eg under, over, around, rising, falling, opening, closing, surrounding, trapping, leading, following).<br>• Time relationships (eg unison, canon, question, answer).<br>• Contact relationships (eg touching, holding, lifting, supporting).<br>• Structural relationships (eg ordering sections of a dance). |

# Glossary

| | |
|---|---|
| **Accompaniment** | The aural environment (eg the sound or music chosen for a dance). |
| **Action** | Basic body actions, including travel, turn, jump, gesture and balance. |
| **Action and reaction** | The influence of one movement (action) upon the movement in response (reaction). |
| **Alignment** | The relationship of body parts to one another. |
| **Appreciation** | Actively viewing dance, in order to describe, analyse, compare and contrast, interpret, make judgements and evaluate. |
| **Breaking** | A form of solo street dance that involves rapid acrobatic moves, where different parts of the body touch the ground. |
| **Canon** | Repetition of movements between dancers, one after another or with each repeat overlapping with the previous one. |
| **Choreographic devices** | Strategies used to create and manipulate movement. |
| **Choreographic intention** | The purpose of the dance; what the choreographer wants to communicate. |
| **Choreography/ Composition** | The creating and forming of a dance. |
| **Complement** | Designing a movement to that it reflects aspects of another dancer's movement, but is not necessarily identical. |
| **Context for learning** | The dance style or theme through which the learning takes place. |
| **Contraction** | Muscular shortening commonly used in relation to an individual movement or body part. |
| **Contrast** | Where movements are different and where they may appear to be opposite in shape, size, dynamic or action. |
| **Copy** | Identical reproduction of material at the same time or at separate times. |
| **Core stability** | Utilisation of the abdominal muscles to provide stability, strength and control from the centre of the body. |
| **Dance style** | A combination of characteristics that distinguish different approaches to moving or choreographing (eg use of music or a distinctive movement vocabulary). |
| **Duet/duo** | A dance performed by two people. |
| **Dynamics** | A quality of movement with reference to time, weight, flow and space (eg the speed, tension). |
| **Embellish** | To make the choreography more detailed, or to decorate a movement to make it more elaborate. |
| **Expressive skills** | Focus, projection and musicality used to communicate thoughts and feelings through movement. |
| **Extension** | The lengthening of body parts. |
| **Focus** | A focal point used by the dancer, directing their vision and increasing communication with the audience. |

| | |
|---|---|
| **Formation** | The shape of a group of dancers (eg line, circle or block). |
| **Fragmentation** | Breaking a sequence into small sections and using parts of it. |
| **Genre** | The category of dance, for example, contemporary ballet or jazz. |
| **Gesture** | A non-weight-bearing movement of the body or limbs to express or emphasise an idea. |
| **Improvisation** | The spontaneous creation of movement without preparation or practice. |
| **Locking** | A style of street dancing that relies on the perfect timing and frequent 'locking' of the limbs, in time with the music. |
| **Mark** | To perform movements without full energy and extension for the purpose of improving movement memory or spacing. |
| **Mirror** | Reflecting the movement of another dancer. |
| **Motif** | A sequence of identifiable movements that communicate the intention of the dance, is repeated, varied and developed throughout; the movements stand out and hold the dance together. |
| **Musicality** | Sensitive awareness to musical phrasing, timing, style and mood. |
| **Narrative** | A storyline or series of events represented through a dance. |
| **Opposition** | The use of an opposite body part to balance the body's movement. |
| **Parallel Position** | The feet, ankles, knees and hips remain vertically in line when standing. |
| **Pathways** | The spatial floor or air pattern along or through which the dancer travels. |
| **Phrase of Movement** | A series of linked movements: a movement sentence. |
| **Plié** | A bending of both the knees, usually ensuring that the knees are in line over the toes. |
| **Popping** | A style of street dance that incorporates the successive rhythmic contractions of the dancer's muscles. |
| **Posture** | When standing, the spine is lengthened while ensuring the shoulders are dropped. |
| **Projection** | The illusion and use of energy to interpret and to communicate the intention of the dance. |
| **Question and answer** | A 'conversation' between dance movements or groups of dancers. |
| **Refine** | To improve the detail and precision of movements when practising the performance of a dance or when creating a dance. |
| **Retrograde** | To reverse a movement or phrase of movement. |
| **Sequence** | A series of movements designed to be performed one after another. |
| **Set sequence/set dance study/set material** | A prescribed sequence of movements usually created by the teacher. |
| **Spatial awareness** | Being consciously alert to your own space, other dancers in the space and the wider space, |

| | |
|---|---|
| **Spotting** | Vision directed towards a focal point (usually a 'point' on the wall at eye level), followed by a sharp turn of the head with the vision returning to that point. A technique used to prevent dizziness. |
| **Stimuli (ideational, kinaesthetic, visual, auditory)** | The idea or concept that inspires the creation of a dance. A springboard for movement (auditory stimuli include: music, percussion, songs, words or poems, ideational stimuli include: idea or story; kinaesthetic include: physical idea, concept or problem; visual include: pictures, sulptures, objects, pattens or shapes). |
| **Syncopation** | The placement of emphasis, with movement, on beats that are not usually emphasised. |
| **Technique** | Physical skills required to execute dance movement (eg posture, placement, alignment). |
| **Transition** | A movement or phrase linking one position or dance phrase to another. |
| **Travel** | Movements that shift from one spatial place to another. |
| **Trio** | A dance performed by three people. |
| **Turn Out** | The outward rotation of the leg, starting in the hip joint with the thighs, knees and feet aligned. |
| **Unison** | Movements performed at the same time by a group of dancers. |

# User Notes for the DVD

- The DVD is compatible with versions of Word 2000 and later.
- The font used may appear inconsistent on some screens. This will depend on individual settings and may also affect the appearance of the font when printed.
- The video extracts can be viewed on most DVD players. When your load the DVD, the title screen will appear. From here, you can click to view user notes for the DVD, or choose to view the menu of units. By clicking on a unit, you will go to a further menu from which you can view the appropriate clip for each task number. At the end of each clip, you are returned to that unit's menu.
- The additional resources of worksheets, teacher prompt sheets and list of resources and contact details are only accessible when the DVD is used in a PC. You can access the folders through My Computer, where you must click on the drive that your comupter is reading the DVD through. At this point, you will see four folders. From here, you can choose to view the worksheets or teacher prompt sheets (both split up into units), the scheme expectations for Key Stage 3, or the list of contacts and references. Double clicking on either of these will open up the folder and will give you access to their content.

## The DVD contains:

- video extacts of phrases of movement for you and your pupils to observe
- pupil worksheets for your pupils to complete
- teacher prompt sheets with information and guidance on the tasks to help you
- an overview of scheme expectations for years 7, 8 and 9
- suggestions for music to accompany your lessons
- a list of references and contacts to help you gain further information.